"God created us wired for sexual pleasure. Our sin complicates God's good gift to us. Bryan Sands reminds us of God's redemption and helps us understand our struggles and desires. I enthusiastically recommend his work which is compellingly written as he addresses what may be the most crucial and controversial topic of today."

> —**Tremper Longman III,** Robert H. Gundry Professor of Biblical Studies, Westmont College, and the author of *God Loves Sex*

"*Everyone Loves Sex* is a honest and human manifesto to redeem the goodness, mystery, and beauty of sex. Using Scripture, story, culture, and science, Bryan Sands courageously lays out a vision for what a new kind of sexual faithfulness could look like."

> —**Steve Carter,** Teaching Pastor, Willow Creek Community Church, author of *This Invitational Life: Risking Yourself to Align with God's Heartbeat for Humanity*

"Bryan nailed it! Finally—an honest, straightforward, and challenging discussion of sex from a godly perspective. Bryan presents the case for faithfulness in a compelling way that truly communicates and reaches the hearts of young people. As a parent of teens, I am so grateful to have this book as a resource. Thank you, Bryan!"

> —**Tom Brooks,** Music Producer (6 Platinum and 12 Gold Albums) and the author of *The Language of Music*

"Living in a culture that prides itself on being so open about the once-forbidden subject of human sexuality, it is shocking how much misinformation is floating around—often in the guise of authoritative fact. Small wonder that even people of faith are frequently confused in their thinking and damaged by their choices. With both clarity in direction and hope for recovery, Bryan Sands brings the light of God's perspective on sex while poignantly and wisely illustrating the reasons behind the principles. Here you will discover that God is not a cosmic killjoy out to limit our fun and restrict our enjoyment, but rather a giver of abundant life who desires his children to experience a great sex life."

> —**Jim Reeve,** Lead Pastor, Faith Community Church, author of *Regenerate: Total Spiritual Transformation*, and television host of *Balance Living*

"*Everyone Loves Sex* is a book that is much needed! In this book, Bryan Sands presents a new approach to talking about waiting for marriage—sexual faithfulness. It's an approach that is relevant to believers and those who do not believe. Instead of simply saying 'just wait for sex until marriage,' this books explains why it makes sense to wait, not only from a biblical perspective but a psychological and sociological perspective. The second part of the book takes a positive approach and encourages the reader to dream of what their life could be. A must read for anyone!"

—**Jurgen Matthesius,** Lead Pastor, C3 Church San Diego and the author of *PUSH: Pray Until Something Happens*

"In this important book, Bryan Sands presents a compelling case, and not just from the Bible, on why waiting for something so good is so right."

—**Vince Antonucci,** Lead Pastor of the Verve Church in Las Vegas and the author of *Renegade* and *God for the Rest of Us*

"With refreshing honesty and unique insight, Bryan Sands invites readers into an important conversation about sexuality. His wise words encourage readers to consider what it means to follow Jesus—not only with our hearts and souls, but with our bodies as well—and, ultimately, what it means to be faithful."

—**Sarah Thebarge,** author of *The Invisible Girls*

"I would venture to say that a person's romantic and sexual choices have the potential to impact their long term health and happiness more than almost any other decision in life. And we happen to live in a time when sexual mores are changing like never before. It's a confusing and tumultuous time for the church as she attempts to discern what 'sexual faithfulness' looks like, yet keep young people in the pews and remain relevant as the culture undergoes drastic changes. At a time when many young adults need more than a simple 'Thus saith the Lord,' Bryan's book presents the scientific rationale behind biblical standards—and how beautiful sex can be in its safest and most glorious context."

—**Melody George**, Director of the Emmy award-winning documentary *End It Now*, and the screenwriter of the upcoming feature film *Your Love Is Strong*

EVERYONE LOVES

SEX

SO WHY WAIT?

EVERYONE LOVES
SEX
SO WHY WAIT?

A Discussion in Sexual Faithfulness

BRYAN A. SANDS

LEAFWOOD
PUBLISHERS
an imprint of Abilene Christian University Press

EVERYONE LOVES SEX
So Why Wait? (A Discussion in Sexual Faithfulness)

LEAFWOOD
P U B L I S H E R S
an imprint of Abilene Christian University Press

Published in association with The Gates Group, 1403 Walnut Lane, Louisville, KY 40223.

Cover design by Caz Sands
Interior text design by Sandy Armstrong, Strong Design
Author photo on back cover by Theresa Cooper Photography

Leafwood Publishers is an imprint of Abilene Christian University Press
ACU Box 29138
Abilene, Texas 79699

1-877-816-4455
www.leafwoodpublishers.com

17 18 19 20 21 22 / 7 6 5 4 3 2 1

This book is dedicated to my beautiful wife Caz!
Without her picking up my slack around the house and
with the kids, this project never would have been completed.
Words cannot express how lucky I am to be married to such a
wonderful, selfless, talented, and generous person. Caz—I am
so thankful that we are on this journey together. Who knows
where it will lead, but it's going to be an exciting ride—and
Abby, Lily-Rose, and I will always be with you!

Acknowledgments

After writing this book, I have realized that it is impossible to write a book without the support of others. The following people have been instrumental and encouraging throughout this process.

Caz—You have been the most encouraging person for me in the process! You always believed in me, always pushed me to get the next chapter done, and always supported me. Thank you for always listening to me pontificate about whatever topic I was writing about.

Students—To all the students who shared their stories, thank you for being vulnerable! Your story will inspire more than you will ever know. And for the students who were part of the focus groups early on, thank you! Your ideas and insight helped shape this book.

Joe Grana—My friend, mentor, spiritual sage, thank you! You have always believed in me, ever since I was a student. You listen to my gripes—and have always been there for me. Thank you for your constant wisdom and encouragement!

Tremper Longman—You are a scholar of scholars, and when I emailed you (while you were on sabbatical), you got back to me. You had no idea who I was, yet you believed in my project and allowed me to ask you question after question. Thank you for being Christlike by showing humility, graciousness, and servanthood.

Tom Brooks—Thank you, Tom, for always believing in me and this project! I never know whether you're touring the world with famous rock stars or here in Orange County, but one thing I can always count on is that you will offer encouragement and inspiration.

Everyone who endorsed my book—Thank you to everyone who took the time, energy, and effort to endorse my book. I am honored that you would look at the manuscript and put your proverbial stamp of approval on it! So thank you: Tremper Longman, Tom Brooks, Joe Grana, Steve Carter, Jim Reeve, Jurgen Matthesius, Vince Antonucci, Sarah Thebarge, Melody George, Paul Angone, Tim Storey, Matt Summerfield, Megan Fate Marshman, Joanna Beasley, Jeremy Jernigan, Gayla Congdon, Tammy Daughtry, Bob Reeve, Darren McMahon, Dan Brooks, and Peace Amadi.

Gayla Congdon—Thank you so much for supporting this book from day one! You always challenged me to keep pushing on because you knew the urgency of this topic. Thank you for wisdom and encouragement.

Melody George—It's been exciting collaborating with you about your upcoming movie, *Your Love Is Strong,* as well as my book. Thank you for your encouragement and expertise.

Paul Angone—Early on in the process you gave me some good advice and inspiration. You have a heart of gold, and I appreciate your friendship!

Mike Goldsworthy—Thank you for encouraging me early on (even though you don't remember it) to have stories to draw the reader in.

Mike DeVries—Thank you for making my content look good—which means I look good! You have been a pleasure to work with—and I have been so impressed with you. If anyone is looking for an amazing editor, contact DeVries: mikedevries@mac.com.

Don Gates—Thank you for saying yes to representing me! You are a fountain of knowledge and just fun to be around. Thank you for believing in me!

Mike Moradshahi—I am so glad we ended up living next to each other for those few years! I was writing this book, you were finishing up your PhD, and we had many late-night discussions about psychology, religion, spirituality, and research. You pushed me to think critically.

Tammy Daughtry—Thank you for always being encouraging and taking a look at the early manuscript!

My parents and brother—Mom, Dad, Thom, all of you have always been so supportive, and that has meant more to me than you will ever know!

Bob Mink—Thank you for reading an early chapter and for your constant encouragement. Thank you for being a great example of a man of integrity.

Rick Harville—When I think of a pastor, you always come to mind. You have the privilege of spending time with professional athletes on a regular basis—yet you still took time out of your day to call me, just to see how I was doing in life and how the writing process was coming along. You are one of the most encouraging people I know.

Evan Money—Thank you for challenging me to write this book!

Jesse Shepherd—Jesse, it has been awhile since you graduated, but I am thankful for our conversations when this book was still in the developmental phases.

My in-laws—I was once told that I was the smartest person in the world because I married a gal whose parents live in a different country! I laughed, of course! I really am thankful to have great in-laws who are supportive of this project.

Ariel Campos and **Spencer Taylor**—You two students are brilliant! Thank you for allowing me to bounce ideas off of you and for your commitment to our Lord.

Contents

Foreword

I remember the day like it was yesterday. I was 13 years old, on my way to football practice in the backseat of my neighbor's van. My buddy Adam and I chatted about the upcoming practice as the music from the radio blared in the background.

Deep in teenage conversation, I couldn't have even told you that the music was on. Yet it only took three seconds of one particular chorus to stop all our conversation and perk up my budding teenage ears like a flower opening to the morning sun.

"*Let's talk about sex, baby . . . Let's talk about you and me. Let's talk about all the good things. And the bad things that may be . . .*" blurted from the speakers as hip-hop trio Salt-N-Pepa filled every crevice in that van—to the great embarrassment of Adam's mom.

It's safe to say that all the faces in the van that day turned bright red as nervous laughter replaced Salt-N-Pepa's famous words. Adam's mom frantically searched for any button on her radio that would cease *all the singing, about all the sex.*

She couldn't find a button fast enough.

Flash forward just *a few* years later, and I can still feel that same gurgling, giggling nervousness rise up and turn my face into a hot tamale as the topic of sex is brought up. And I'm married with three kids now!

What is it about sex?

What is it about the topic that feels either completely taboo and off limits, or sung about in the most explicit of details?

Sex is either addressed like an *Andy Griffith* episode (so basically not at all), or portrayed like an episode of *Girls* or *New Girl* (the focus and core desire of every character on the screen).

What is it about sex that brings out this vast range of emotions, feelings, paradoxes, and awkward conversations?

Well, maybe it has to do with people doing stuff together naked. I mean, two people just playing croquet naked would be the talk of the town.

Yet, maybe there's more to it than all the nakedness. Maybe it's because of the vast range of emotions, feelings, and paradoxes that arise when we discuss another word—a word with which sex is typically intertwined like a giant pretzel.

That word? Love.

Like sex, no other word in human language has been more misconstrued, mistrusted, celebrated, worshipped, and cursed than love.

Love cures us and makes us sick, sometimes in the same look. Love has stopped wars and started them. Love leads some to wait for sex and leads others to rush into it.

To make love. I mean, that's often how sex is described, especially when we want to wax poetic about it. Like two people coming together in that scene from *Ghost*, where they're making it rain while somehow making a clay pot, all at the same time. They don't teach that move in premarital class.

Yet is sex love? Maybe that's the real question.

Maybe just like an impossible *Kama Sutra* move, making love equal sex will leave you flat on your face.

Maybe for many of us, sex has become the easiest escape from love—easing all our insecurities, fears, and pains into a moment of escape that does nothing to alleviate our pain. No, most likely it only heightens the pain once the deed is done. Sometimes sex rips apart love rather than strengthening it.

Love, sex—we need to talk about all of this. Or better yet, let's see what Bryan Sands has to say about why everyone loves sex. Bryan masterfully mixes and bridges the psychological, sociological, religious, and the practical to begin a conversation about "sexual faithfulness."

Bryan doesn't explore the topic of sex in a heavy-handed, condemning way. Nor does he shy away from the awkward realities and details that rarely enter the church walls. Bryan tells it like it is and shows how much God and science have to say about sex, and how, surprisingly, they agree more than we realize.

Sex is how life begins. Yet for many, sex can also feel less than life-bringing.

How do we do sex right? (And I'm not talking about positions.) How do we become sexually faithful in a world that feels faithful to so little?

> **Share This**
> Sometimes sex rips apart love rather than strengthening it.
> #everyonelovessex

How do we let sex become the most beautiful aspect and act of love that God has ever created for us?

Well, let's talk about sex, baby.

—Paul Angone, author of *101 Secrets for Your Twenties* and *All Groan Up,* and creator of AllGroanUp.com

Sex, Science, Redemption, and Your Future

Everywhere we look, we see it, from television and movies, to the Internet and social media. We are surrounded by sex. The average age a person first views pornographic material is twelve.[1] By the time college students graduate, 72 percent have hooked up with at least one person.[2] *The Penguin Atlas of Human Sexual Behavior* even estimates that sexual intercourse happens 120 million times a day on planet Earth.[3] More than facts and numbers, what does all this really tell us?

Sex is one of the most powerful forces in the world. Whether you have experienced the physical act or not, you intuitively know there is something powerful about sex. As you read the pages ahead, you will read stories of students just like yourself—students longing for connection with others. When the connection is not there, people search to fill this kind of longing in many different ways. Some seek it in revolving-door relationships. Some seek it in sex.

This is not your typical book on waiting for marriage. This is not a book about how awful sexuality is or how sex is "sinful." It's not. This is a book about love, about faithfulness, about making decisions about our sexuality that give us the best possible chance to enjoy it to the fullest. It is a book about the longings and needs we all have and where we seek to find fulfillment. Along the way you will hear stories from students like yourself, some with more sexual experiences than they care to recount and others with little to no experience. It is a book about real people. Let me start by sharing my story.

Like many people, I made one of those "wait until I'm married" commitments when I was in high school and was given a bracelet as a physical reminder of that commitment. On our wedding day, I cut the bracelet off and gave it to my wife, Caz. You can see the video of me cutting the bracelet off at our wedding at https://www.EveryoneLovesSex.org/media. I am proof that sexual faithfulness is possible.

I have had people comment that this sort of commitment is impossible—and I suspect some question whether or not I actually followed through on my commitment. The reality is this: while I did indeed make good on my commitment in high school, I did not actually wait until I was married to have sex. Let me be vulnerable.

The summer before my ninth-grade year of high school, I met a girl. Well, I actually met six girls. They were sitting in front of a local Del Taco. Armed with a small notepad and a pen, I approached the girls and asked them for their numbers—all six of them! To my surprise, they gave them to me!

One of those girls was Sarah.

Later that night, I stayed the night at a friend's house. He had his girlfriend over, who happened to know Sarah. We made arrangements for his girlfriend and Sarah to come over. We had one thing on our mind. And I remember asking for forgiveness in advance for what I was about to do.

Sarah came over around 1 A.M. and we just lay on the floor for a while. My heart was pounding and I was nervous. I had just met Sarah hours ago and here we were lying next to each other, knowing we were about to hook up. After I got the courage, we hooked up, and she and her friend went home.

The next day my friends showered me with praise and encouragement. It was as if it was a rite of passage for me. But looking back on that event, I felt nothing. There was no magical moment, no connection, and no fulfillment, just a hookup. Because I was so young and immature, I did not understand how to handle what had happened, so I avoided Sarah. Looking back on it, I am sure I caused her a lot of emotional hurt.

So when I write about issues of redemption and change, I write about it from firsthand experience. That is why I am so passionate about sexual faithfulness. When we are not sexually faithful, we can hurt not only ourselves, but also others. However, it is never too late to commit to sexual faithfulness. The following year I made my commitment to sexual faithfulness—and followed through with it. That moment, standing in front of Caz, was powerful. It was powerful because of my story, my struggles, my decision to change—and God's redemption. What he did for me, he can do for you as well.

Whether your story is similar or different, God offers redemption. You may have caused yourself or others a tremendous amount of hurt; however, now is the best time to change your actions. We may not be able to change the past, but we can reshape our future. God can and will bring you healing. It may take longer than you want, but he is there with you. Sexual faithfulness is something that you can always commit to, regardless of the past. We are not prisoners to the past; we can be something different, something new.

Redemption

One of the most pervasive themes we discover in the Bible is that of redemption. Redemption is God taking the first step to act compassionately on behalf of the powerless. In the New Testament, it is clear that redemption begins with God identifying with our shortcomings and brokenness. First, he was able to identify with all of our shortcomings and brokenness because he lived life as we do. This means Jesus knows what it is like to struggle. He knows what we are up against. Second, he went to the cross in order to set us free from sin and death, so that we could live the life we were always meant to live.[4] The writer of Hebrews puts it this way:

> Now that we know what we have—Jesus, this great High Priest with ready access to God—let's not let it slip through our fingers. We don't have a priest who is out of touch with our reality. He's been through weakness and testing, experienced it all—all but the sin. So let's walk right up to him and get what he is so ready to give. Take the mercy, accept the help. (Heb. 4:14–16 *The Message*)

Regardless of your past, God has redeemed you. It is up to you to receive his redemption—to "accept the help." The reason we do not have to worry about our salvation is because Jesus redeemed us by his death, burial, and resurrection. We are set free from all our sins—past, present, and future. However, the reason we need to "accept the help" is that we are in the process of mending our relationship with God. When we come to the Lord for healing, he redeems us—and begins the process of changing us to live into that redemption. As we seek God daily, our redemption transforms us—and that is where our freedom comes from.

A Biblical Story of Redemption

Do you remember the story of the woman caught in adultery in John 8? It has been observed that the scene was a conspiracy in order to challenge Jesus and see what he would say. In other words, the group of men conspired against the woman, so that when she slept with a married man, they would "catch her" in the act and bring her to Jesus. (Oddly, these men only brought the woman—not the man.) Jesus' response, however, was nothing they could have imagined. He said that whoever is without sin should be the first to throw a stone. John tells us the men walked away one by one, the oldest first, then the youngest. *The Message* finishes the story this way:

> The woman was left alone. Jesus stood up and spoke to her. "Woman, where are they? Does no one condemn you?"
>
> "No one, Master."
>
> "Neither do I," said Jesus. "Go on your way. From now on, don't sin." (John 8:9–11 *The Message*)

In this account we see the love and forgiveness Jesus offers everyone on display. The religious leaders really did not care about the woman; she was just a means to an end. They were using her to bring some charge against Jesus because they wanted him out of the picture. She was of no concern to the religious leaders—but she was to Jesus. You are loved and cherished regardless of your choices. It is never too late and you are never too far outside of God's redemption to embrace sexual faithfulness. It is *never* too late to accept the redemption Jesus has to offer.

Sexual Faithfulness and Your Generation

The millennial generation is no stranger to strong opinions on sex.[5] We intuitively know the power of sex and its various benefits. The connection and pleasure sex brings those who engage in it are well known. Movies are produced, books are written, and the physical act itself is sought out by many every day. But what if in our search for connection and sex, we end up missing out on so much more? What if in the end, our frantic pursuit of sexual fulfillment actually works against the very desires and needs we want fulfilled? As we journey together, we will discover that sex is much more than the physical act. Sex is a bond—one that strengthens, comforts, and builds safety and trust among its partners. Our bodies long for physical touch, but we also long for something more—something deeper. When we treat sex casually and as only a physical act, we potentially miss out on something so much greater.

It is because sex is something so much more than the physical that I am committed to spreading the message about sexual faithfulness. Sexual faithfulness is being sexually faithful to your future (or current) spouse. In the past, terms like "sexual purity" or "sexual abstinence" were all the rage, but those phrases sadly miss the point and do not do an adequate job of communicating the purpose, gift, and beauty of sex.

They miss out on the deep interweaving of God's gift and the science of sexuality.

Each of the following chapters invites us to explore a different aspect of sexuality. As we journey together, we will discover what lies behind our needs and desires—and what our lives *could* be if we choose sexual faithfulness. We will hear from real people sharing their real experiences and raw emotions. There are stories of joy and struggle, desperate longing and deep fulfillment, regret and redemption. Our hope is that these stories from your peers will begin to remove the mask from sexual fulfillment and allow us to see what our passions and desires are truly all about.

> **Share This**
>
> As we journey together, we will discover what lies behind our needs and desires–and what our lives *could* be if we choose sexual faithfulness.
>
> #everyonelovessex

Section One of this book is entitled "The Purpose of Sexual Faithfulness." More than the tired "just don't do it because the Bible says" platitude, we will search for that "something better"—a holistic vision of waiting until marriage—sexual faithfulness. As we investigate this theme across the psychological and sociological worlds, we will gain a fresh vision of what it means to be created in the image of God and see how this overarching narrative can guide our decisions regarding our sexuality. Utilizing the latest studies in psychology, in Chapter One we will uncover the sometimes hidden emotional implications of sexual activity before marriage. Our journey will take us deep into the power of the brain—our command center—to learn about the influence of various chemicals released during sexual activity, chemicals that create a lasting emotional imprint and bond us to one another. This bond can be a positive one of connection, or it can leave us in a negative state of bondage—feeling emotionally connected to another beyond the boundaries of the relationship. Against the backdrop of real-world experience, Chapter Two explores what current sociological research has uncovered in regard to what happens when one tries to find connection and love in casual sexual encounters, and how counterproductive it can be in helping individuals or couples find a place to belong and be loved.

In Section Two, entitled "The Vision of Sexual Faithfulness," we turn our attention to two primary desires—the need to be loved and the need to be in community—and why they are as deeply felt as they are and their impact on our sexuality. We will explore how these desires often get translated into the pursuit of sexual experiences to find fulfillment. As we will see through personal stories and experiences, sexual encounters never truly fill those voids. But how can we truly pursue love and community in ways that are life-giving? What might a life look like that is set on the pursuit of these things, including sexual faithfulness?

> **Share This**
>
> As we will see through personal stories and experiences, sexual encounters never truly fill those voids.
>
> #everyonelovessex

Purpose, Hope, and Vision

I have two purposes in writing this book. First, to share current research from different scientific disciplines that sheds light on why we do what we do. There are reasons why we have the longings and desires that we do and, more importantly, why we search for them in sexual fulfillment. The second purpose of this book is to encourage, bring hope, and cast vision of what our lives could look like—lives based on love, connection, community, belonging, and faithfulness. These are the basis for meeting our deepest needs and longings—and what set us up to ultimately enjoy and connect with others through our sexuality.

As you read this, you are somewhere on a spectrum of sexual experience. Some of you have had years of sexual experience. You may even have had more experiences than you wish to remember. On the other side of the spectrum are those with little to no sexual experience, and who may wish they could be sexually experimenting. And there are yet others—those who have been violated and have had unwanted sexual experiences and are still dealing with the hurt.

Wherever you are on the spectrum, there's hope! There's hope for those who have had many sexual encounters, and there's hope for those who are not sexually experienced to find someone to fall in love with and grow closer to every day. There is also hope for those who have been violated. No one has the right to commit such a horrendous act—and no one deserves, nor did they do anything to deserve, being violated in that way. For those in the midst of pain and hurt, there is hope as well.

Wherever you are in life, this book is for you. Yes, this book is about waiting for marriage, bringing a completely different perspective than what you may have heard before. This book is also about the future, one in which you are in charge of your destiny—a future filled with hope and connection, where faithfulness is central, and where you can help others. The reason I believe all this is because I lived it. It's my story—filled with dreams and desires, and heartbreak and redemption. Sure, it may have ended well, but it didn't start out that way.

Your future is up to you—and your journey begins here. Allow this book to be the catalyst for what your life could be. Start making the choices now that will make the vision of your future a reality.

Along the way you will be challenged—and you may have to wrestle with your past. Hopefully this book will be a conversation partner, and a guide to help you through the process. My desire is that this book might be a beginning to help you through the process of deciding what you will do with your future. It is true that everyone loves sex, so let's find out why—and perhaps why the decision to wait could be the best decision you ever make.

CONTINUING THE DISCUSSION

1. What were your initial thoughts on these statistics given at the beginning of the introduction?

   a. The average age a person first views pornographic material is twelve years old.

   b. By the time college students graduate, 72 percent have hooked up with at least one person.

   c. *The Penguin Atlas of Human Sexual Behavior* estimates that sexual intercourse happens 120 million times a day on planet Earth.

2. Do you believe sex is one of the most powerful forces in the world?

3. Did Bryan's story resonate with you? Why or why not?

4. How do you define *redemption*? What does redemption look like in your life?

5. How would you define sexual faithfulness?

6. Do you feel this book will encourage you to wait for marriage and redemption? Why or why not?

Have you shared your thoughts online yet?
#EveryoneLovesSex

Notes

[1] Miranda A. H. Horvath, Llian Alys, Kristina Massey, Afroditi Pina, Mia Scally and Joanna R. Adler, *"Basically . . . porn is everywhere": A Rapid Evidence Assessment on the Effects that Access and Exposure to Pornography Has on Children and Young People* (London: Office of the Children's Commissioner, 2013).

[2] Sharon Jayson, "More College 'Hookups,' but More Virgins, Too," *USA Today*, March 30, 2011, http://usatoday30.usatoday.com/news/health /wellness/dating/story/2011/03/More-hookups-on-campuses-but-more -virgins-too/45556388/1.

[3] *The Penguin Atlas of Human Sexual Behavior* is cited by Matt Rosenberg at About.com, http://geography.about.com/od/culturalgeography/a /geographyofsex.htm.

[4] "Redeem, Redemption," *Baker's Evangelical Dictionary of Biblical Theology*, http://www.biblestudytools.com/dictionaries/bakers-evangelical -dictionary/redeem-redemption.html.

[5] Millennials are those born from around 1980 to around 2000.

SECTION 1

The Purpose of
Sexual Faithfulness

According to the biblical creation story, God created the land and the sky and all that they contain with a spoken word. Everything was just as planned—it was good. When the story gets to the creation of humanity, however, something truly astounding is mentioned: humanity is created in the image of God. This means each of us is a representative creation of God. No matter who we are, we have value. We are unique, special. The apostle Paul, knowing our created and undeniable value in the eyes of God, writes to the Corinthians. He reminds them that their bodies are the temple of the Holy Spirit and that how they choose to use their bodies is a reflection of that created image. When we live counter to who we have been created to be, there are dangerous implications psychologically and sociologically. This first section will explore the way in which we have been created, how we reflect the image of God, and what impact this has on our sexuality. More than the tired "just don't do it because the Bible says" platitude, we will paint a vision of something better—a holistic vision of waiting until marriage—sexual faithfulness.

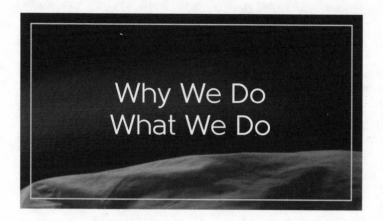

CHAPTER 1

Why We Do
What We Do

Why Do People Have Sex?

Answering the question "Why do people have sex?" may seem kind of laughable. I mean, just about anyone with a pulse could list dozens or more reasons why people have sex in a matter of minutes. Yet strangely, this has not always been the case.

If we went back in time, say a couple of hundred years ago, and asked the same question, we would hear one of three classic responses. First, you might hear something about being in love. Second, you might hear something about procreation. The third response would be "because it feels good." Add those up and you have the "the big three"—but as we said, that was then and this is now.

Now if we asked that very same question today—to your friends—we would get a full spectrum of reasons why people have sex—way more than just "the big three." Everything from love to pleasure, from connection and intimacy to a desire to be wanted, and beyond. While sex itself may be the same, the reasons for having sex seem to have expanded over time.

What's fascinating about sexology (yes, that is the *official* term for the study of sex—believe it or not, this is a thing) is that sexologists (again, an actual profession) have discovered that we are wired to have sex.[1] In other words, as human beings, sexual activity is hardwired into our being; it is something that is natural—and needed—for the well-being of the human race. But that still does not fully answer a central question: *Why do we do what we do?* Why has our culture shifted so much in answering the question, "Why do we have sex?" That's what we want to explore.

> **Share This**
>
> In other words, as human beings, sexual activity is hardwired into our being; it is something that is natural–and needed–for the well-being of the human race.
>
> #everyonelovessex

You see, there really is a reason why we do what we do! There is a reason why we search for connection and intimacy in sexual encounters, even though we know we may regret it. There is a reason why we are willing to go against our morals. Let's start with Drew.

Why Drew Did What He Did

I have known Drew for close to five years. And oddly, over those five years we've been friends, I'd never heard him tell his entire story. I'd heard bits and pieces here and there, but never the whole thing—and never like this. Drew had sought me out, asking if we could get together. He knew I was writing this book and said that he wanted to share a little about his story. I knew he had a story to tell, but I did not know how big it would be—and I did not know how much of his past played into his life decisions. Not knowing what I was in for, I set up our meeting at a local Starbucks, because, hey, everyone needs a little extra caffeine pick-me-up in the afternoon.

"Bryan, you mind if we sit outside?"

"Sure." In a matter of minutes, I knew exactly why he asked.

Even though Drew's parents were married seventeen years, his parents did not have the ideal relationship. Constant fighting and arguments were a regular part of growing up for Drew. His dad would often leave the house and go to strip clubs to drink and watch the dancers. What Drew did not know was that his dad was also cheating on his wife. On a number of occasions, Drew would have to go into these bars to drag his passed-out dad home. His father was also physically abusive to both Drew and his mom. One day, fed up with not receiving love and positive attention, his mom decided to also have an affair. Needless to say, Drew's family dynamics were not going to win any awards.

In order to seek refuge, Drew pursued sexual encounters with multiple girls while in middle school. Truth be told, his first sexual experience was when he was eight years of age. An older girl seduced him to have sex with her. (As he started to open up and share about his middle-school experiences, I thought to myself, *If I didn't know him, I would think he was seriously making all this up*.)

"I enjoyed and cared about the relationships I was in. I mean, I wasn't out just trying to hurt certain females, but before I got too emotionally attached, I would push them away before I got hurt. Seeing the hurt my parents went through was something I didn't want to go through."

At the age of seventeen, Drew's parents divorced, and even though there was massive conflict in the home, the divorce still really hurt him. Instead of seeking professional help to heal his wounds, Drew sought out solace in multiple relationships. He continued having sex with multiple girls as a way of escape.

> **Share This**
>
> I just desired to be wanted–but at the same time I would push females away. I was scared of being hurt."
>
> #everyonelovessex

"I made a vow to not follow in my dad's footsteps, but here I was doing the same thing. I thought these sexual encounters would eventually bring me healing. I was always trying to be loved. I did want a family— still do want a family—but I was trying to fill that void. I just desired to be wanted—but at the same time I would push females away. I was scared of being hurt."

I could see Drew process his past decisions before my eyes. Even though he is currently doing well, he was still dealing with those past decisions and their impact. Hearing him relive his hurts and decisions, I was visibly shaken.

But the story didn't end there.

Drew was tired of being hurt—so he decided to never let it happen again. Rather than being the recipient of hurt, he would make sure that he did what he wanted, when he wanted, and to the degree he wanted. This decision led him down a long road of self-destruction, alcoholism, and drug use. By the time Drew graduated high school, he did not have any respect for women; he just wanted to conquer them.

After high school, Drew had a decision to make: go to college or the military. He chose the military, and quickly found a group of friends to party with and girls to sleep with. During this period of life, he felt good—or so he thought at the time.

But the pattern of sleeping around, alcoholism, and drug use that he continued throughout his military career finally caught up with him—and ultimately he paid a price. He was given a "general discharge under honorable conditions"—an act of grace bestowed on him by the military judge.

After the military, Drew and a friend hung out at strip clubs. It was at a strip club that he met the girl who would give birth to his two children. Drew was twenty-four years old. Their relationship did not last, and Drew continued his sexual activity with women, even with his two young children in the picture. When he was ordered to take custody of his children, he had to conceal his drug use, sexual activity, and alcohol use from them.

One day, Drew was having a family barbecue; he was smoking and drinking. His daughter, seeing him with a cigarette in one hand and a bottle in the other, asked, "Dad, are you doing drugs?" Hearing her say that broke his heart. In a split second, he saw himself through the eyes of his child and realized that he needed to change—if not for himself, then for his kids. He admitted that he looked to alcohol, cigarettes, and sex as a way to cope with life, a way to escape. At that barbecue, he made the decision to give up alcohol and cigarettes—but not his sexual exploits.

Six months after the barbeque, while sitting at his girlfriend's house, Drew made a decision that he would refrain from sleeping around. Drew really loved his girlfriend and wanted to commit to sexual faithfulness to honor the Lord and his girlfriend. He wanted to do the right thing, and he was committed to that decision.

> **―Share This―**
> He admitted that he looked to alcohol, cigarettes, and sex as a way to cope with life, a way to escape.
> #everyonelovessex

"That same day, however, I went out and had sex. I just took her for granted, telling myself she would always be there. Weeks later, she found out I had cheated on her—and she was gone."

Hearing the emotion in Drew's voice was revealing. He still regrets the moment he went back on his word. It still haunts him. I know Drew. He is resilient, strong, and a man of his word. I think even when his life was out of control, his word was important; so for him to break his word was demoralizing.

One day his children's biological mother asked, "Why do you always have to have a woman around you?" For whatever reason, it was that moment when he realized sex was something he needed—that he was in fact a sex addict. Over all the years, from the time Drew was in middle school all the way to the beginning of his thirties, he never thought of himself as a sex addict. Drew is now able to look back and realize he was a sex addict and an alcoholic. When he attempted to count the number of girls he had slept with, Drew estimated the number to be above three hundred.

Drew has been in counseling and recovery groups throughout the years, and credits his healing to his relationship with Jesus, the community in support groups, and the counselors who have walked with him through the years. Seeing him today, no one would know how intense his story really is. Today, Drew has full custody of his children, a full-time job, and volunteers at his church and children's schools.

Why You Do What You Do

As we look deeper at Drew's story, some elements appear as to why he did what he did. Drew never had a secure relationship growing up, and he never experienced what a healthy relationship looked like; consequently, when sexual relationships started turning into something more relational, he ran. Because relationships always meant turmoil—and that was something he couldn't handle.

Drew had a ton of emotional turmoil, starting from his childhood, and he will be the first to say that does not excuse his behavior. But looking back on his life, Drew expressed on a number of occasions that he was always trying to fill a void. It wasn't until years later that he discovered fulfillment and joy come from community and a relationship with Jesus.

Why do we do what we do? Why do some people sleep around? Perhaps it's because we're trying to fill a void in our lives caused by hurt, pain, or insecurities. Why do some people watch porn? Perhaps it's because we're trying to bypass the fear of rejection or because it's a way of feeling "connected" to something. Why are some people afraid of relationships? Perhaps we're afraid of attachment or rejection or failure. Why do we sometimes live with the guilt of past decisions?

There is a reason for every one of the scenarios we just discussed. No one wakes up one day and says, "You know, I want to sleep with three hundred people!" No one wakes up and says, "Today I want to have my relationship go bad!" The reality is that our past often affects our current situation if we do not choose to go in a different direction.

Wherever we are in life, we always have the power to choose! We can always choose to find healing—or we can choose to continue our course. For many of you, the very fact that you are

> **—Share This—**
>
> Wherever we are in life, we always have the power to choose! We can always choose to find healing—or we can choose to continue our course.
>
> #everyonelovessex

reading this book is a declaration that you want to choose a different path. And if that's the case, you are headed in the right direction. No matter what you did in the past or why you did it, God will always love you—just the way you are.

There's Always Hope: One of the aspects of this book is to offer you resources. If you're ready to see a counselor, for whatever reason, go to www.aacc.net. Or if you're in Orange County, California, you can go to www.DrHenslin.com.

If My Office Walls Could Talk

I have worked with students in middle school and high school, young adults, and families directly for fourteen years, and since 2011, I have worked directly with college students. Needless to say, I have had many conversations about life. Over the past six years, I estimate that the majority of students who came to talk with me did so because they were struggling. Whether it is depression, anxiety, attention deficit disorder, eating disorders, struggles at home, thoughts of suicide, or a host of other issues, with a little help and guidance, students can often see exactly why these issues started occurring.

When Stephen came into my office because he was cutting himself, it turned out he did not know how to handle the abuse his family put him through years ago. Even though the police and courts were involved, the pain was still there. Over time, he just wanted to feel something—anything—instead of feeling numb and dead inside. And so he started cutting. When those endorphins were released in his body, he felt a sense of calmness and peace come upon him. But that feeling only lasted for a little while. As he met with a professional counselor, he was able to get to the root of cutting—and has not cut in the last three years.

When Sandra first came to my office, she was struggling academically and needed help. It quickly became clear that she had felt alone and on her own most of her life. Her parents were not engaged with her life, and she was left to figure out what life was all about. She started to improve, but then she disappeared for a few months. After those months went by, she stopped by my office and told me she moved in with her boyfriend, got pregnant, and had an abortion—she even showed me the paperwork. She was always trying to find a place to belong—and moving in and sleeping with her boyfriend gave her a sense of belonging.

When Alan came and chatted with me, he said he'd had thoughts of suicide on and off since he was in high school. I met with him and encouraged him to see a counselor and to go back to his psychiatrist. After a change in his medication, he came back to my office and I immediately noticed a difference. I asked him what happened, and he told me that once they made the medication change, he was a completely different person.

So, why do we do what we do? It seems that if we look long and hard enough, we can begin to see the reasons that lie behind our actions, and choices begin to emerge. With the help and support of our family, or a community of people, or a trusted counselor, we can begin to unpack some of the reasons why we make the choices that we do. It is only when we uncover these reasons—and bring them into the light—that we are able to make true and lasting changes, ones that will bring hope and healing.

My hope is that this book begins that journey for you. No matter where you are or what choices you have made that led you to that place, I hope you will begin to explore the reasons why you do what you do. My hope is that you will have the courage to bring those into the light and begin to make lasting changes in your life, ones that will allow you to live the life you were created to live.

This is not a book about how sex is "sinful, awful, and dirty—so save it for the one you love and want to spend the rest of your life with." Seriously, that's terrible. Rather, this book is about the amazing gift sex is. I'm not here to judge or condemn anyone; far from it. I want to paint a picture of what sex can be, what your life can be.

> **Share This**
>
> I'm not here to judge or condemn anyone; far from it. I want to paint a picture of what sex can be, what your life can be.
>
> #everyonelovessex

I have this crazy idea that God actually is a big fan of sex—after all, he is the one who created it in the first place. So let's go on a journey together—a journey where we will discover what sex is really all about. Why do people have sex? For a lot of differing reasons—reasons that make sense when we stop to take a good look inside.

But to make sense of it all, we need to go all the way back to the beginning—to see what God was envisioning when he created the gift we call sex.

CONTINUING THE DISCUSSION

1. Before reading this chapter, how would you have answered the question, "Why do people have sex?" How do you answer it now that you have read the chapter?

2. Was Drew's story difficult to believe? Do you know anyone like Drew?

3. Have you ever asked yourself why you do what you do? Why do you feel the need to _____ (fill in the blank)? Share.

4. Do you believe that no matter what you have been through, there is always hope? Why or why not? How have you experienced hope?

5. Remember, this is not a book about how sex is "sinful, awful, and dirty—so save it for the one you love and want to spend the rest of your life with." Do you find that refreshing? Why or why not?

6. Do you know why you do what you do?

> Have you shared your thoughts online yet?
> #EveryoneLovesSex

Note

[1]Kelli Miller, "The Top 20 Reasons People Have Sex: Sexual Motives Go Far beyond the 'Big Three'—Love, Pleasure, and Making Babies," WebMD, February 16, 2012.

CHAPTER 2

Bonding or Bondage?
(The Psychological World)

How Maddy Was Betrayed

Anyone who has been betrayed knows its sting! And Maddy's betrayal was still stinging when we met. After hearing her story, I was so overwhelmed that I asked if she would elaborate on it for my wife, Caz, and me. She agreed and asked if she could bring a friend along for moral support. "Absolutely," I told her. The story she told that day over coffee is one of heartbreak and loss, of longing and need. I'm sure she is not alone. As she told us her story, I could tell that the pain was still fresh and that she was still in the process of making sense of it all. Here is what she told us.

"I think it all started because Enrique and I had similar backgrounds." Both of their mothers were the breadwinners of their household and both of their biological fathers were abusive, Maddy's verbally and Enrique's physically. They were both the oldest in their families and felt the responsibility of taking care of their younger siblings as well as bringing in some money. Maddy shared with us that she learned so much about his family history and his view on life that it brought comfort knowing that he understood what it was like to struggle.

After a few months of getting to know each other, Maddy and Enrique confirmed their interest in each other. Although she had some trust issues with guys, Maddy felt she could trust him—especially because she could relate to the drama they both had been through with their families. Trying to be a gentleman, Enrique expressed to Maddy that he did not want to make things "official" quite yet. He wanted to take his time and make sure that it was the right decision. Maddy respected his outlook and waited patiently.

After two years of patience and some self-discovery, Enrique and Maddy had officially become a couple—and things progressed fairly quickly from that point forward. As their relationship started to progress emotionally (as well as physically), she was hoping that this void in her life would be filled. The void, as she is able to reflect on it now, was there because her biological dad was verbally abusive and her relationship with her mom was rocky. She was longing for something stable, something comforting.

Maddy looked forward to her eighteenth birthday—the mark of being an adult, or so she thought. Growing up, Maddy felt ready for adulthood because she had witnessed so much of it through her mom's struggles. She had this idea in her head that once she turned eighteen, her childhood problems would just disappear.

Turning eighteen meant Maddy was ready for the next step, not only in life, but also in her relationship with Enrique.

After some time in solitude and reflection on where they stood in their relationship, Maddy felt that this decision was what would unleash a real, adultlike love. In her train of thought, Maddy had considered all possible reasons why she shouldn't sleep with Enrique and tackled them with reasons of why it was okay to take it to the next level. The reasons, Maddy expressed to us, included the following:

> *I've known him almost my whole life.*
> *We can relate to one another.*
> *I know he will not hurt me.*
> *We share common interests.*
> *I want to spend the rest of my life with him.*
> *God will bless me for considering all of these factors.*
> *I waited all this time to make this decision.*
> *I am wise for waiting as long as I did.*
> *All my friends lost their virginity at such a young age.*
> *I'm the good one of my friends; I waited this long.*

After much thought and consideration, Maddy decided it was time. The night she lost her virginity to Enrique, Maddy remembers falling asleep and pondering, *Is this it? No sparks? No magic?* Maddy had the "sex talk" as a kid, but it never included what she might feel like emotionally, especially after the first time. Even her friends, who had multiple sex partners, described details of what to expect, but none of that pertained to her. "I knew that Enrique loved me, but I wondered why the act of losing my virginity to him did not take me to the next level emotionally." She wondered, "Why are we not emotionally healthier now?"

As time went on, they began arguing—arguing not only about petty issues, but also about important ones. They fought so often that Maddy became confused about why she felt so connected to him when they would have sex—but then immediately feel miles away afterwards. The heart-wrenching part for Caz and me to hear was when Maddy expressed that all the years they were together, Enrique never really valued her or cared for her emotionally. When she tried to express her feelings over the years, it only angered Enrique, so she stored away these feelings in fear of losing him.

Many hurtful things began to surface. She started discovering lies he would tell her about his whereabouts. She learned of his flirtatious behavior with other girls—and saw text messages he had exchanged with girls he was interested in. As their relationship progressed, it began to solely consist of arguments, betrayal, and rejection. It was soon to end—but not before she announced some big news to Enrique.

The First Relationship Story: Adam and Eve

In the very first line of the Bible, we learn that God created the heavens and the earth, and ultimately created all that is in it. We also find that he created humanity—male and female—in his own image. The text goes on to tell us how God entrusted this newly created paradise to Adam, saying, "Take care of it." One of Adam's first tasks was the naming of the animals, and he gave them names as he saw fit. Each had a mate. Each had someone—a companion. All seemed well, but there was a problem in paradise.

Adam was alone.

Even though he had God and all the animals, Adam wanted a partner—another like him. To relieve this loneliness, God created another like him—Eve. Now in this paradise, we have partners, Adam and Eve, who work together to tend to the land, care for the animals, and who enjoy each other in every way. They were able to look at each other in full vulnerability and not feel any insecurities or shame. It was God, Adam, and Eve living in the Garden of Eden—a picture of perfect harmony, perfect intimacy, and perfect unity.

Sadly, it would not last long.

God had created a tree in the Garden of Eden—the tree of knowledge of good and evil. God encouraged them to enjoy everything in the land because it was created for them, but one thing he asked was that they not eat from the tree. One simple request.[1]

They could have enjoyed everything; all they had to do was stay away from that one tree in the middle of the garden. One day, Eve was by the tree, and a serpent asked if she wanted to taste the fruit. Eve refused at first, saying God had told them not to eat the fruit from the tree. The serpent explained that the only reason God told them not to eat of it was because they would become like God himself. God is holding back on you, says the serpent. He is not fully trustworthy.

Harmony hung in the balance. What would they do? Choose to trust God—or themselves? Needless to say, they chose to eat of the fruit—and then everything changed.

After all this, Adam and Eve no longer had the same intimate relationship. They now felt shame, insecurities, and deceit. They realized they were naked and ran and covered themselves, hid from God, and blamed each other for what happened. Their intimate bond of unity, of oneness, had been shattered. Now their world became what God had never intended. These two, for the first time, were at odds with each other—their deep abiding connection lay on the ground in shattered pieces.

The Story within the Story

The story of Adam and Eve is our story. It is the story of our desires, our choices, and the brokenness we all feel. It is the story of what we all yearn for: a deep, intimate, meaningful, trusting relationship with a partner—oneness. This is how God created us. This is his desire for us as well. The question is this, however: Is it possible for us to get back to that oneness?

God made Adam out of the dust of the ground—and then breathed his Spirit into him—the breath of life. Genesis records the account this way, "Then the LORD God formed a man from the dust of the ground and breathed into his nostrils the breath of life, and the man became a living being."[2] The creation of Eve is different: "God caused the man to fall into a deep sleep; and while he was sleeping, he took one of the man's ribs and then closed up the place with flesh. Then the LORD God made a woman from the rib he had taken out of the man, and he brought her to the man."[3]

So we have Adam created from the dust of the ground and Eve created from Adam. God did not create Eve out of dust—but out of Adam's rib. But why did God create Eve in this way? The concept behind creation from a rib points to the closeness and intimacy these two would share, a creation unlike any other. The phrase "bone of my bones [rib of my ribs] and flesh of my flesh" (Gen. 2:23) is not only a physical attribute, but a relational one as well. The Hebrew word for *rib* is never used this

> **Share This**
>
> "Woman was not taken from man's feet as if she were beneath him or from his head as if she were over him, but from his side, as an equal with him," so that they may walk side by side.
>
> #everyonelovessex

way throughout the rest of the Bible—only in the creation account.[4] Early interpreters would later note, "Woman was not taken from man's feet as if she were beneath him or from his head as if she were over him, but from his side, as an equal with him,"[5] so that they may walk side by side. God instituted unity between Adam and Eve, creating them to bond with each other, encouraging them to have sex not only for procreation but also for the joy of it! Humanity was created to be able to bond—emotionally, spiritually, and yes, even physically.

> **—Share This—**
> During sex, two beings—two souls—are uniting, becoming one. There is an intimacy and deepness unlike any other act.
> #everyonelovessex

In Genesis 2:24–25, the dynamics of marriage are introduced, noting that a man will leave his father and mother and be united to his wife, that the two would become "one flesh." The word "one" is the Hebrew word *echad*. *Echad's* basic definition is, you guessed it, "one." But it also has a deeper significance. *Echad* carries the idea of one in the midst of unity, and it is closely connected with another Hebrew word that means "to be united."[6] The Hebrew word for "flesh" is *basar,* and it can mean "flesh" or "body," among other things. When these two words are combined, it paints the picture of this couple being united at the deepest level, not only physically, but also emotionally and spiritually.[7] Husband and wife, one made from the elements of dirt, the other taken from a rib, now enjoy God's gift of sex—a physical unity that envisions the becoming of one flesh once again—emotionally and spiritually. As Adam and Eve came from one body, now they would, once again, become one.[8]

Echad–Unity in Singularity

Let's investigate how echad is used in other parts of the Bible so we can understand the richness of its meaning:

- In Exodus 24:3, Israel was entering into a covenant with God using the word echad, "with one voice," meaning all of Israel (the unified one) was entering into the covenant.
- In Judges 20:8 and 1 Samuel 11:7, echad is used in the sense of one nation uniting to take action against injustice.
- Ezekiel predicted that the two split kingdoms would once again become one, echad, by symbolically joining together two sticks (Ezek. 37:17).[9]

Echad is the same Hebrew word used in the Shema, "Hear, O Israel: The LORD our God, the LORD is one" (Deut. 6:4). This is the basis of our monotheistic faith. The richness of *echad* highlights that God is unified. When we talk about the Trinity, we use language of one God revealed in three persons, and signify that these three "persons" are the one God. The idea is unity within the one. During sex, two beings—two souls—are uniting, becoming one. There is an intimacy and deepness unlike any other act.

It is interesting that the writer of Genesis 2 connects this sense of oneness—*echad*-ness—within the dynamics of marriage. It is as if to communicate that this bond is so powerful, so transcendent, that marriage is the only force that can contain it.[10] The writers of the Hebrew Scriptures clearly understood this. They honored the importance of marriage so highly that the groom was released from his occupation for an entire year.[11]

Think about it. No work stresses. No fears of being drafted. No term papers or homework. The couple simply had each other to focus on. Marriage was sacred.

As we investigate this deep bond created during sex, we see that this *echad*-ness is not only something we find in the biblical text, but also something that has been recognized in psychology. Psychologists agree that sex is a powerful force, and the misuse of it has deeply negative implications in our lives. This deep emotional, physical, and spiritual bond created within sex is also acknowledged in the world of psychology. Scientists have discovered that a chemical called oxytocin creates this kind of bond.

Science and Spirituality– Empirical Meets the Spiritual

During sexual activity, our brain releases a number of chemicals. Some of the chemicals include estrogen (the chemical that gets a woman in the mood), norepinephrine (the chemical that is like adrenaline and creates the palpitating heart), dopamine (the "got-to-get-it chemical"), vasopressin (the "monogamy chemical"), and the chief of all these chemicals, *oxytocin* (the "cuddle hormone" or "love hormone").

Think of oxytocin as glue, promoting bonding and attachment. If all the hormones had an opportunity to vote for the "most popular" hormone in the yearbook, oxytocin would win every time, because it makes others feel good and close when it is active. It has been dubbed the "cuddle hormone" or "love hormone" because it does simply that. Oxytocin creates bonding, trust, and generosity in us.[12] In fact, whenever you feel comfort or security, you can thank oxytocin. Every form of human bonding, from nonsexual to sexual interactions, involves oxytocin to some degree.[13]

Oxytocin is also involved in childbirth, breast-feeding, and in interactions like hugs or kisses, increasing trust and empathy. The other crucial time oxytocin gets released is during sex. Released in the brain, this hormone creates an emotional bond between partners.[14]

One of the prominent figures in neuropsychology, Dr. Daniel Amen, is involved in cutting-edge research and has helped millions of people have healthier brains, which translates to healthier lives. One of the parts of our brain Dr. Amen writes about is the "deep limbic system," located near the center of the brain. It sets the emotional tone of your mind, tags events as internally important, stores highly charged emotional memories, and controls appetite and sleep cycle, among other things. In his book, *Change Your Brain, Change Your Life*, Dr. Amen notes:

> Whenever a person is sexually involved with another person, neurochemical changes occur in both their brains that encourage limbic, emotional bonding. Yet limbic bonding is the reason casual sex doesn't really work for most people on a whole mind and body level. Two people may decide to have sex "just for the fun of it," yet something is occurring on another level they might not have decided on at all: Sex is enhancing an emotional bond between them whether they want it or not. One person, often the woman, is bound to form an attachment and will be hurt when a casual affair ends. One reason it is usually the woman who is

hurt most is that the female limbic system is larger than the male's. One likely consequence is that she will become more limbically connected.[15]

Whether we like it or not, oxytocin creates a bond between you and your partner; and the more sexual encounters you have together, the stronger the bond. When oxytocin is released, it also floods the brain with endorphins, a natural opiate that activates the pleasure center in the brain. When combined with vasopressin (the "monogamy chemical"), the release of oxytocin will "create vivid emotional, sensory memories, which in turn deepens feelings for the love object."[16] Oxytocin can also bring a couple closer together, create that feeling of happiness when "your song" plays, and even make you prefer your partner's shape, smell, and overall appearance above all.[17]

> **Share This**
>
> Whether we like it or not, oxytocin creates a bond between you and your partner; and the more sexual encounters you have together, the stronger the bond.
>
> #everyonelovessex

In other words, oxytocin is a type of chemical bonding glue.

A person may choose to have sex once or many times with many different people, and whether they know it or not, a bond is formed each and every time. When this bond gets broken, it creates pain. It leaves a void. Sound familiar? Have you ever felt a deep sense of hurt or pain after a breakup? Ever felt a hollow void after a one-night stand? Do you find yourself repeatedly playing the scenario in your mind, maybe even thinking of different outcomes? Believe it or not, there is a chemical reason for all this. Chances are you are doing these things because of the intoxicating attachment that was created between you and your partner when you were sexually involved. The emotional attachment that is created during sex, resulting from the release of oxytocin, binds two people together.

Investigating the Psychological Side

One of the first things every student learns in an introduction to psychology class is the basic definition of psychology. "Psychology is the scientific study of behavior and mental processes and how they are affected by an organism's physical state, mental state, and external environment."[18] In other words, psychology explores our past and present circumstances in order to understand why we are the way we are—and then attempts to bring us back to a sense of wholeness.

One of the most crucial components to psychology is a clear understanding of how our brain functions. The brain is our command center; it sends messages to all the parts of our body so we can function. The brain is one of the most powerful organisms in the universe and controls everything about us. In fact, the brain will store information from events that happened years ago—and until we deal with any residual pain, they will remain there, locked away.

The reason memories come up when we hear a song is because of the power of our brain. The reason we are anxious or depressed is because of our brain. The reason we are impulsive is because of our brain. Therefore, psychologists study the brain and how certain events affect our emotional well-being. Scientists have even studied the brain in regard to one's first sexual experience—and as we will see, psychologists have confirmed that sex is as powerful as we read in the beginning chapters of Genesis.

The Power of Your First Sexual Experience

Do you remember your first sexual experience? It is more than safe to say you probably do. I bet you can even remember the who, what, when, where, and why of the encounter—not to mention the overall feeling of it. Regardless of how many months or years in the past this sexual encounter took place, you most likely still remember it. Maybe there is even a song, a smell, a place, or a thought that will trigger your memory of your first sexual experience. Have you ever asked yourself, "How come I can remember all those details, yet cannot remember what I ate for dinner two nights ago?" The answer has to do with psychology and the complex inner workings of your brain.

Young adults' brains are at the peak of their ability to release chemicals—chemicals that can encourage everything from reckless behavior to exploring new adventures. This high level of chemical release leaves one susceptible to being molded by one's first sexual experience. Researchers have extensively studied the implications of one's first sexual experience—and the results are quite literally staggering!

A researcher analyzed data from a longitudinal study (a study that stays with the participants through a number of years) on more than 1,600 pairs of siblings from the ages of fifteen to twenty-nine. The researcher divided the constituents into three groups pertaining to the timing of their first sexual experience:

1. *The Early Group*: Those who had sex for the first time at or before the age of fifteen.
2. *The "On-Time" Group*: Those who first had sex between the ages of sixteen to nineteen.

3. *The Late Group*: Those who waited until twenty years of age to have sex.

While the data of the "early" and the "on-time" groups showed no appreciable differences, those who did not have sex until at least the age of twenty showed significant findings. "[This group] earned more money, acquired more education, had fewer partners and reported far fewer problems with their marriages."[19]

There are many different potential reasons for this finding. It may be because an adolescent had good parenting (and listened to it), learned the value of delayed gratification, was highly selective, had high religious/moral values, or maybe was just scared to have sex while a teenager. It could also be that those who had their first sexual experiences in the late group were spared from those awkward sexual teenage experiences that can leave deep emotional wounds. The answer depends on the individual.

Regardless of the reasons, this study demonstrates the power of sex from a psychological point of view. Again, it goes back to the Garden of Eden: sex creates a deep intimate bond—spiritually and physically. When we confuse the order of sex first and then a deep intimate relationship, we are going against how we were designed. Science is demonstrating the powerful bond everyone can have with a partner.

---Share This---
"[This group] earned more money, acquired more education, had fewer partners and reported far fewer problems with their marriages."
#everyonelovessex

Science of Love: A True-or-False Quiz[20]

1. Women find men who wear the color red most attractive.[21]
2. Carrying a musical instrument doubles your chances of scoring a phone number.[22]
3. The body part that makes a woman most attractive to men is her breasts.[23]
4. Eye makeup is better than lipstick for boosting your sex appeal.[24]
5. Men who marry younger women live longer.[25]
6. Going out with a big group of friends makes you appear more good looking than if you go out with a couple of friends.[26]
7. Men who smile are sexier than those who do not.[27]

Rats, the Smell of Death, and a Young Adult's First Sexual Experience

Scientists have also tested the power of sex on rats. A group of scientists sprayed sexually receptive female rats with a chemical called cadaverine, an odor of decaying flesh, and placed them in a cage with male virgin rats.[28] They also placed virgin male rats and sexually experienced female rats *not* sprayed with cadaverine in another cage. After they placed the scented female rats into the cage, they placed virgin male rats ready to rumble in the same cage. In case you are wondering, rats are not fond of the smell of decaying flesh—they abhor it. However, the virgin male rats did not let the smell of death stop them from having their first sexual experiences. In this experiment, the male rat's first nine sexual experiences were either with female rats smelling of a deathlike odor or (in the other cage) female rats smelling like a normal rat (whatever a normal rat smells like).[29]

Here's where this experiment gets fascinating! For every male rat's tenth sexual experience, the male rats and the scented and unscented (that is, those who did and did not smell like death) female rats were placed in an open field and had the freedom to rumble with whomever they chose. It was a literal "lovefest." The male rats that only had sex with unscented female rats prior to this experiment "pursued the unscented females selectively and ejaculated exclusively with them."[30] However, the male rats whose previous nine sexual encounters had been with the scented female rats—sought after both the unscented and scented female rats.[31] These rats did not discriminate in any way, shape, or smell!

The Point of Rats, Death, and Sex

Scientists are empirically proving that sex is powerful, especially the first sexual experience. In fact, your first experience can influence your sexual preferences in the future.

> It is becoming increasingly clear that there is a critical period of sexual behavior development that forms around an individual's first experiences with sexual arousal and desire, masturbation, orgasm, and sexual intercourse itself. During this period, the sensory and motor mechanics of the behavior become integrated and crystallized along with the development of preferences for ideal activities and physical features of a partner.[32]

During one's first sexual experience, there are a number of chemicals being released for the very first time—and at such high levels that our bodies actually yearn for that same experiential state. The reason we can remember so much of that first experience is because of all the physiological events that occurred inside our brain. In the case of our rats, their first sexual experience molded their associations—even associating the smell of decaying flesh with sexual excitement.

If we go back to Genesis 2, we read about God giving humanity this special gift of sex so couples could bond on a physical and spiritual level. If a married couple's first experience is with each other, we see how special and powerful this bond can be. But if one's first sexual experience is random (which tends to happen in our culture today), there is a good chance there will be implications for further sexual encounters.[33]

> **Share This**
>
> During one's first sexual experience, there are a number of chemicals being released for the very first time–and at such high levels that our bodies actually yearn for that same experiential state.
>
> #everyonelovessex

Fear of the Positive

One afternoon, Maddy was feeling sick at the smell of food and decided to rush to the store to get a pregnancy test. She took the pregnancy test, although there should have been no reasonable concern because she was on birth control and hadn't missed a day. Maddy explained to Enrique that she was going to take a test just to reassure herself that she wasn't pregnant—and that he shouldn't be worried because she had been diligent in taking her birth control pills.

Though she tried to remain calm, Maddy was trembling at the thought of possibly being pregnant. She sat in his bathroom and prayed to God that the test would come back negative. After a few short moments of prayer and waiting for the results, she removed the test, and her heart sank.

Positive.

"This is impossible! I took my birth control pills!" She took a second test to be sure.

Again, *Positive.*

Maddy opened the bathroom door and walked toward the couch where Enrique was sitting. He looked up at her and asked what the results were. "It says I'm pregnant."

Enrique's expression was that of a blank stare. Maddy said he seemed "calm and unbothered." She asked him if he was okay, and he said, "I'm fine. Let me take you home, though, because it's late."

The car ride was silent and awkward. Maddy wondered, "How is he so calm right now when I am freaking out? Does he not care?" As they walked to her house, Maddy used the opportunity to ask him what he thought. "Enrique, do you not care? You haven't said one word to me."

He shook his head and responded, "I'm fine, Maddy. You can do whatever you want, and I'll support your decision. I'm not ready to have a child and neither are you, but it's your body, so it's your decision. I'll support whatever you choose." At this point it was clear where Enrique stood on whether or not he wanted the baby to be born. He seemed not to care—at all.

The next morning, Maddy awoke certain of the fact that she did not want to have a baby. Her rationale was that she was too young and not ready—not to mention that they were not even on the best of terms to raise a child. Consequently, she decided that she would go against everything she believed and have an abortion. When she told Enrique, he was relieved.

Maddy began to take the necessary steps to follow through with the procedure. She explained to Enrique the fee that would be charged to do this; he made it clear that he could not contribute financially, so Maddy would have to pay the expenses alone. After the procedure, Enrique picked her up and took her to his house so that Maddy could rest. Maddy slept off and on for most of the day because she was emotionally drained and heartbroken.

Enrique lay next to her the majority of the afternoon, but seemed disconnected. He was on his phone texting the entire time while Maddy faced emotional turmoil and physical exhaustion. Maddy asked him who he was texting, and without any shame he told her the name of the same girl Maddy caught him cheating with. She felt the sting of his betrayal and lack of concern.

As Maddy lay there in bed, feeling defeated, humiliated, and angry because her boyfriend was interested in someone else, she couldn't feel anything but disgust toward him. Though she had been instructed by doctors not to drive, she picked up her things and drove home. She had tried to make this relationship work, had tried to make responsible decisions, had tried to work through his cheating—even looking the other way when she knew what he was doing. What she was hoping for was someone to fall in love with, to share life with. What she ended up with was pain, brokenness, betrayal, and emptiness.

Trust—and Don't Settle

The serpent came to Eve, saying, "God doesn't want you to eat the fruit because you will be like him."[34] And she listened to him. She listened to his deceitfulness. What exactly was that lie? It was that God was not trustworthy, that he was holding out on them.[35] That there was a better way! Ever since Adam and Eve ate of the fruit, nothing has ever been the same. Still to this day we believe the same lie. We believe, "God doesn't know what is best for me. God doesn't care about my deepest desire. God isn't there!" Here's the essential question we must ask: "Is God truly trustworthy?"

Psychology and Scripture are on the same page in regard to sex. Sex is a gift—an incredibly powerful gift—but one that best functions within a specific context, a context to be recognized, honored, and one that brings us closer to our spouse and our Creator. Two themes in the Song of Songs are absolutely clear: sex is good, and one should not engage in it impulsively or prematurely.[36]

It is evident from creation onward that we are wired to bond, a point that has been verified by psychology. Secular and religious psychologists both agree that we are designed to bond. When people choose to take that step of sexual faithfulness, they are setting themselves up for success and fulfilling relationships. Ask yourself: *What could my relationship look like if I do not settle? What would my emotional life be like if I did not sleep around?* Regardless of your past or current situation, you can always choose to be sexually faithful from this point on.

CONTINUING THE DISCUSSION

1. What was the most impactful part of the chapter for you? Why?

2. Could you relate to Maddy's story? Why or why not?

3. Have you ever heard the Adam and Eve story told this way? What was the most significant part for you? Why?

4. Explain the Biblical concept of "one flesh."

5. What was most significant for you in regards to the power of oxytocin?

6. What are your thoughts regarding the association between substance abuse and multiple sex partners?

7. If in a group study, does anyone feel comfortable talking about a personal story of the power of sex? If reading alone, do you have a story of the power of sex?

8. Was there anything about the psychology behind sex that you disagreed with? What and why?

Have you shared your thoughts online yet?
#EveryoneLovesSex

Notes

[1] Let's not be quick to assume that we would not have chosen like Adam or Eve. Also, the reason God created the tree they were not to eat from was to give Adam and Eve a choice. In order for true love to exist, there must be a choice. Without choice, it is simply coercion.

[2] Genesis 2:7.

[3] Genesis 2:21–22.

[4] Walter C. Kaiser Jr. et al., *Hard Sayings of the Bible* (Downers Grove, IL: IVP Academic, 1996), 94–95.

[5] Ibid.

[6] R. Laird Harris et al., *Theological Wordbook of the Old Testament* (Chicago: Moody Press, 2003), 60.

[7] I am thankful to Old Testament scholar Dr. Tremper Longman III for his insights on this topic over lunch on May 21, 2015.

[8] John H. Walton and Victor H. Matthews, *The IVP Bible Background Commentary: Genesis–Deuteronomy* (Downers Grove, IL: InterVarsity Press, 2000), 20.

[9] Harris et al., *Theological Wordbook of the Old Testament*, 60.

[10] I appreciate John Mark Comer's thoughts on this concept. For more information, see John Mark Comer, *Loveology: God. Love. Marriage. Sex. And the Never-Ending Story of Male and Female* (Grand Rapids: Zondervan, 2014).

[11] Deuteronomy 24:5.

[12] Tori DeAngelis, "The Two Faces of Oxytocin," American Psychological Association, February 2008, http://www.apa.org/monitor/feb08/oxytocin.aspx.

[13] Judith Horstman, *The Scientific American Book of Love, Sex and the Brain: The Neuroscience of How, When, Why, and Who We Love* (San Francisco: Jossey-Bass, 2012), 23.

[14] Earl Henslin, *This Is Your Brain In Love: New Scientific Breakthroughs for a More Passionate and Emotionally Healthy Marriage* (Nashville: Thomas Nelson, 2009), 9–12.

[15] Daniel G. Amen, *Change Your Brain, Change Your Life: The Breakthrough Program for Conquering Anxiety, Depression, Obsessiveness, Lack of Focus, Anger, and Memory Problems,* revised and expanded (New York: Random Harmony, 2015), 94.

[16] Henslin, *This Is Your Brain In Love,* 11.

[17] Ibid., 9–11.

[18] Carole Wade and Carol Tavris, *Psychology,* 6th ed. (Upper Saddle River, NJ: Prentice Hall, 2000), 1–2.

[19] Matt Huston, "Sex: Can't Hurry Love," Psychology Today, January 2, 2013, http://www.psychologytoday.com/articles/201303/sex-cant-hurry -love.

[20] Quiz and answers come from Dr. Melissa Lem, who appeared on the *Steven and Chris Show* on the Live Well Network, http://livewellnetwork. com/Steven-and-Chris/episodes/The-Science-of-Love/9469270.

[21] True! In a 2010 study from the *Journal of Experimental Psychology,* men who wore red were rated as more powerful, attractive, and sexually desirable. Studies also show that men find ladies in red to be more eye-catching. Scientists think the crimson hue is a biological signal for sexual excitement, since the effect also occurs in nonhuman primates like baboons.

[22] True! A 2013 study from France had a twenty-year-old man ask women on the street for their phone numbers. Thirty-one percent of women gladly gave him their digits when he was carrying a guitar, but only 14 percent when he was empty-handed. Men who post online profile photos of themselves holding a guitar are three times more likely to have their friend requests accepted. Researchers believe that musical ability could be a sign of better genetics and intelligence, so forget the sports car and buy a guitar!

[23] False! A 2011 study from New Zealand analyzed men who looked at pictures of the same woman digitally altered to have different breast and waist sizes. Although men spent the most time gazing at her breasts, the model's waist-to-hip ratio was what determined her attractiveness, irrespective of cup size! A waist that measures 60 to 80 percent smaller than the hips is considered most appealing.

[24] True! Volunteers in a 2003 study from the *International Journal of Cosmetic Science* rated five different pictures of the same woman in order of attractiveness. Men ranked a full face of makeup as most attractive, followed by just foundation, and then just eye makeup. After no makeup at all, lipstick only was rated as least attractive. So if you are running out of time before a date, science says to focus on your skin and eyes and skip the lips!

[25] True! A 2010 German study showed that older men who married younger women were up to 20 percent less likely to die, and the greater the age gap, the lower the risk. Unfortunately, the opposite applies to women: marrying a considerably younger or older partner increased their risk of death by up to 30 percent! One theory is that younger women encourage older men to stay active and social, but wives with younger husbands are less socially accepted, leading to more stress and worse health.

[26] True! Research from California in 2013 revealed that men and women were found to be significantly more attractive when seen in a group of four or more as compared to alone. This "cheerleader effect" or "sorority girl syndrome" is likely caused by a trick of the brain: when we see a face in a crowd, it appears more like the group's average, which humans typically find more attractive than outliers.

[27] False! Happy guys apparently finish last. In a 2011 study from the University of British Columbia, women rated photos of proud and brooding men as more sexually attractive than their happy, smiling counterparts. Scientists suspect that pride communicates better status and resources, while a grin could indicate neediness and desperation. Interestingly, men in the same study found smiling women significantly more attractive. So guys, if you are looking for a fling, practice that moody look, and ladies, a smile is your best accessory!

[28] James G. Pfaus et al., "Who, What, Where, When (and Maybe Even Why)? How the Experience of Sexual Reward Connects Sexual Desire, Preference, and Performance," *Archives of Sexual Behavior* 41.1 (2012): 31–62.

[29] Ibid, 47.

[30] Ibid.

[31] Ibid.

[32] Ibid., 32.

[33] Be sure to keep reading, because I write about the importance of redemption and healing for those who have had sexual experiences before marriage. You are not doomed to failure or regret for the rest of your life. And if you have had sex before marriage, that does not disqualify you from having amazing sex with your spouse in the future. Wherever you are, make wise decisions from here forward. That is committing to sexual faithfulness.

[34] Genesis 3:5 (paraphrase).

[35] Comer, *Loveology*, 24.

[36] Dan B. Allender and Tremper Longman, *God Loves Sex: An Honest Conversation about Sexual Desire and Holiness* (Grand Rapids: Baker Books, 2014), 17.

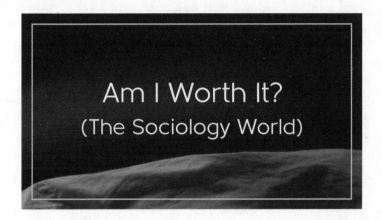

CHAPTER 3

Am I Worth It?
(The Sociology World)

When Needs Are Not Met: Brooklyn's Story

Brooklyn's story is one of those kinds of stories that if anything could go wrong, it did. When she was in the sixth grade, Brooklyn's grandmother, the anchor of the family, passed away. Everything seemed to change overnight. Brooklyn's mom became severely depressed and turned to drugs in order to cope, while Brooklyn's stepdad continued in his alcoholic ways.

Late at night, Brooklyn's mom would often sneak out to go to the neighbor's house, her drug dealer, to get high. After a while, Brooklyn's mom and the next-door drug-dealing neighbor started having an affair. It was her way of numbing the pain of an alcoholic husband and the loss of her mother. It was a way to hide—and to feel loved.

After a few months of being "functionally dysfunctional," a new normal began to take hold. Brooklyn would often stay the night at her best friend Sarah's house. Sarah's mom, Elizabeth, was also best of friends with Brooklyn's mom. One night, Brooklyn, her best friend Sarah, and Sarah's brother, Jackson, all slept in the same bed. It was a small house and not uncommon for them to share beds. In the middle of the night, Brooklyn awoke to Jackson molesting her. Startled, Brooklyn ran to the bathroom and had no idea what to do, so she just stayed there.

The next morning Jackson acted as if nothing had happened, like everything was perfectly normal. Brooklyn said nothing. Brooklyn felt her only recourse was to push it aside as if it had never happened. And that is exactly what she did.

In seventh grade, Brooklyn's stepdad came home unexpectedly and walked in on her mom and the drug-dealing neighbor sleeping together in their house. Brooklyn's stepdad broke into the room and punched him multiple times, throwing him around the room. Brooklyn's mom yelled for Brooklyn to get her two younger brothers and keep them away from the room. Being the older sister, Brooklyn locked all of them in the room farthest from the fighting. The boyfriend ended up bloodied, bruised, and with three broken ribs. Brooklyn witnessed everything.

Brooklyn's stepdad sold the house without his wife (soon to be ex-wife) knowing, and left. Sometime later, the police came to the door, letting them know they were being evicted. So Brooklyn, her mom, and her two brothers were now living from hotel to hotel. But this, too, would soon change. In living from hotel to hotel, her mom's drug use and lifestyle started to catch up to her. One night, her heart started to fail and she had to be rushed to the emergency room. In the emergency room, Brooklyn's mom was pronounced clinically dead for six minutes—but was revived. It was the first time Brooklyn had ever prayed to God.

With her mom recovering, it was not possible for her to take care of the children; consequently, they all moved in with Brooklyn's stepdad. While they were living with her stepdad, Brooklyn's situation took a turn for the worse. His anger had worsened and his bouts of drinking had become more severe. He would force Brooklyn and his biological son to play drinking games. If they declined, he would verbally and even physically abuse them. Whenever he got angry, he would physically and verbally abuse Brooklyn in particular. Since Brooklyn's mom was still very weak, there was not much she could do.

As Brooklyn's eighth-grade year progressed, she became severely depressed and suicidal—she even attempted to take her own life. She started cutting herself and became bulimic. For various reasons, memories of being molested at the hands of Jackson resurfaced in her mind. Having had enough of the battle in her mind, one day she called a meeting with Jackson and his parents. Jackson's dad looked Brooklyn in the eyes and said, "I don't blame my son for what he did—look at how you dress!" Jackson, of course, denied the whole thing. Jackson's mom, knowing the truth of what had happened, sat silently. She did not want to jeopardize her friendship with Brooklyn's mom.

> **Share This**
>
> As Brooklyn's eighth-grade year progressed, she became severely depressed and suicidal—she even attempted to take her own life.
>
> #everyonelovessex

When Brooklyn told her mom about the meeting sometime later, her mom did not believe her. Brooklyn's emotional state and well-being kept getting crushed. She tried to find love and comfort, but kept coming up empty. She felt worthless.

While she was in tenth grade, Brooklyn was at a party and lost her virginity to a classmate who had a girlfriend at the time. Shortly thereafter, she met Carlos.

Carlos was a drug dealer, and he taught Brooklyn all about drugs. They dated for about a year. When Brooklyn got into eleventh grade, Carlos cheated on her with Brooklyn's cousin, Heather. Carlos would often compare the two sexually, saying Brooklyn would do this good—but her cousin, Heather, would do this other thing better.

"That still affects me to this day," Brooklyn told me.

Brooklyn spiraled deeper into a life of drugs, alcohol, and sex. Whenever she would try to confide in her mom, seeking love and support, her mom would always take someone else's side.

> **Share This**
> Brooklyn spiraled deeper into a life of drugs, alcohol, and sex. Whenever she would try to confide in her mom, seeking love and support, her mom would always take someone else's side.
> #everyonelovessex

As she approached her senior year of high school, Brooklyn started getting her life together. After graduation, she moved out to the beach. One day she decided to start attending church. She started mentoring teenage girls who were going through the things she went through—yet at the same time she also decided to move in with her next boyfriend. This was short-lived, as he was soon deployed overseas.

When she turned nineteen, Brooklyn started working at Victoria's Secret, and it was there that she met Michael. Shortly after meeting each other, they decided to move in together. Brooklyn wanted to surprise Michael on his birthday. She really wanted to show him how much she loved him, so she prepared a surprise party for him with all of his friends. Brooklyn took him out to a special lunch and then came back to their place, where he was greeted by all of their friends.

At the party, he got angry with Brooklyn because he felt she was not paying enough attention to him. Brooklyn was doing her duty as host and making sure the party was flowing smoothly. Michael pulled her aside and said, "You're not paying enough attention to me; you're talking to everyone else, and I'm over it. You and I are done."

Brooklyn was crushed. She left to clear her head, and then came back. When she came back, Brooklyn found Michael in their bedroom with one of Brooklyn's co-workers passed out on their bed. Michael explained to her that nothing happened. Brooklyn was livid and said, "How dare you have another girl sleep in our bed—and be in our room alone with her!"

Shortly after the party, Brooklyn continued to feel worse about herself. After all, how else could she feel? Her self-esteem dropped; she also felt like a hypocrite. She was still involved with her church, trying to help the young girls, but kept going back to guys who were bad news. Still hurting from Michael and wanting to get back at him, she started sleeping with his best friend, Andrew. There was no romance, no feelings, just sex and revenge. One day, however, she received news that would change everything—she was pregnant. She was twenty years old.

When Brooklyn brought up the pregnancy, Andrew coldly replied, "I don't care what happens to the baby. You knew what we were doing was just for fun. I don't know what you expect from me, but I want nothing to do with the baby."

Brooklyn decided to have an abortion. Andrew drove her to the abortion clinic. The clinic gave Brooklyn two pills that would terminate the baby. Andrew drove her back to his mom's house. "I have to go to work. My mom can look after you." And with that, he left. Brooklyn decided to drive herself home, where she took the pills. "The abortion was an all-day process. I was crying the entire day, making frequent visits to the bathroom, and during one of those visits, I saw the fetus I had aborted. Andrew never checked up on me."

Brooklyn was at the lowest point in her life. Racked with guilt and pain, her thoughts started getting the best of her. As she shared how she felt all those years ago, my heart broke for her. Over and over in her head she was thinking: *No wonder people treat you like they have! You just killed a baby! You deserve everything that has happened to you! You're a horrible person and deserve nothing but hurt and shame!*

> **Share This**
>
> Over and over in her head she was thinking: *No wonder people treat you like they have! You just killed a baby! You deserve everything that has happened to you! You're a horrible person and deserve nothing but hurt and shame!*
>
> #everyonelovessex

Sociology and What Every Person Needs

Sociology is the study of human social relationships and institutions. Sociology's subject matter is diverse, ranging from crime to religion, from the family to the state, from the divisions of race and social class to the shared beliefs of a common culture, and from social stability to radical change in whole societies.[1]

One of the great discoveries in dealing with relationships is a theory proposed by Dr. Abraham Maslow called "The

Hierarchy of Needs." Famously displayed in the form of a triangle with the most basic needs being at the bottom, the theory explains that one cannot move to a higher level on the triangle until you have your needs met on a lower level.

The first level in the hierarchy of needs is physiological needs. Physiological needs are the basic physical necessities needed to survive. These necessities include oxygen, water, and food. These needs must be met before one can move to the next level. The second level is safety and security needs, including shelter, a peaceful environment, and so on. The third stage is love and belongingness. This stage demonstrates the importance of relationships, platonic and romantic, as well as the need to belong—to matter. The fourth stage is the need for self-esteem, and the fifth stage is self-actualization.[2]

This chapter deals specifically with the third stage in the hierarchy. It is interesting that after the first two stages are met, which are physical, the next most important stage is one that focuses on relationship—love and belonging. If you feel a sense of belonging, you also feel that you are worth belonging—that you are worth it. The sad fact is that many people today do not feel they belong; consequently, they do not feel they are worth anything. Each of us has an innate desire to belong—to love, and to be loved. However, as we especially look at our actions, are we setting ourselves up to progress relationally and emotionally or are we setting ourselves up for failure? Let's look at some areas where we are trying to find fulfillment of a deep need—but are going about it in ways that are harmful and destructive.

> **Share This**
> Each of us has an innate desire to belong—to love, and to be loved.
> #everyonelovessex

Are Hookups the Best Way to Find Love and Belonging?

With the cost of college constantly rising, many parents cannot afford to pay college tuition for their children; consequently, the burden of paying for school is often left on the shoulders of the student. This means students are not only taking a full class load, but also have to work to pay for school. Additionally, with the competition that naturally arises in the university setting, students know that in order to get ahead, getting good grades is not enough. Students also have to participate in or lead extracurricular activities, like being on the debate team, serving as a student leader, leading service projects in the community, being involved in an internship, and anything else that will look impressive on a résumé or application.

The stress and time constraints on students can feel crushing at times. For many students, it is impossible to even think about a serious, committed relationship. As some students have said, "A relationship is like taking a four-credit class," and "I could get in a relationship, or I could finish my film."[3] Many young adults have come to the conclusion that a traditional relationship would be too much to handle, that it would "cost" too much. Therefore, instead of finding a "traditional relationship," students will often opt for the hookup in order to get their physical needs met.[4]

Add into the mix social media, college students trying to "find themselves," and living in close proximity, and what results is a recipe for a hookup culture. Somewhere between 60 to 80 percent of American college students have participated in some type of hookup experience,[5] and one survey indicated that 79 percent of young men and 73 percent of young women approved of premarital sex. To put that into perspective, in

1943, 40 percent of young men approved of premarital sex, while only 12 percent of young women approved.[6] Times have indeed changed.

Not too long ago if a guy were interested in a girl, he would ask her out on a date. And if he really wanted to impress her, he would bring flowers. Perhaps even yellow roses, symbolizing that he wanted to work on their friendship before anything else. On the date, he had better have opened the door every time they got in the car and walked on the part of the sidewalk closest to oncoming traffic to protect her. Even before he arrived to pick up his date, he had to call her home phone, and the chances were high (if she lived at home) that he would have a conversation with her mom or dad before she got on the phone. (Apparently, picking a girl up for a date was not as easy as texting her that you are there to pick her up . . .)

Alexis's Story

Alexis is a tall, attractive junior who was taking a full load of classes, was on the debate team, was involved with stressful internship interviews, and had pressure to be at the top of her class. Needless to say, she did not have time for a traditional relationship. Occasionally, when her work was finished, Alexis would text her regular hookup buddy and have sex. She was not even that impressed with the guy's personality. There was no relationship, no expectations—just sex. She would always go over to his place, she said, because she did not want to wash the sheets. Whenever she showed up at his doorstep, there was always alcohol to get the evening started.[7]

Today, students claim dating is becoming a thing of the past. One student boldly stated, "You just don't date at colleges."[8] Another said, "In a big way, hookups have kind of taken the place of—not exactly eclipsed—relationships, but hooking up is kind of an easier way for college students to act on their sexual desire without making a big commitment."[9]

It is obvious that students hook up because of the physical, but I am always interested in what is beneath the physical. What is it that causes a person to hook up with a stranger or an acquaintance? When we dig deeper, we see not only through scientific studies but personal interviews with college students that a big part of hooking up is because the partners long for something emotionally deeper—they want to be loved and to belong. They want to know they have worth. In fact, over a quarter of men and nearly half of women indicated they desired a romantic relationship to follow a hookup. However, less than 10 percent of women and men actually expected a hookup to evolve into a traditional romantic relationship.[10] Though many students desire to be in a traditional relationship, they do not know how to be in one because many never have.[11]

There seems to be something innate in all of us, a longing for something deeper, something meaningful. In a relationship, there is safety and commitment, and studies—along with personal interviews and conversations—seem to be pointing to that conclusion. "It is likely that a substantial portion of emerging adults today are compelled to publicly engage in hookups while desiring both immediate sexual gratification and more stable romantic attachments."[12]

When we look beneath the surface of hooking up, we notice the act is partially about creating a close connection with someone. It is not surprising when we look at the large number of young adults hooking up, since we are wired for that type of intimacy. We are wired to be in community and to feel worthy to belong to that community. Relationships and connection with others are part of living healthy lives. The main concern, however, is *if we are wired to be in relationships, and have the desire for sex, is hooking up the best way to develop healthy relationships, both romantically and platonically?*

What researchers are coming to understand is this: hooking up actually deepens the emptiness people feel to be loved and belong. In a study of 1,468 undergraduate students, participants reported a variety of consequences after a hookup:

- 27.1 percent felt embarrassed
- 24.7 percent reported emotional difficulties
- 20.8 percent experienced loss of respect
- 10.0 percent reported difficulties with a steady partner[13]

In another study, students self-reported:

- 78 percent of women and 72 percent of men who had uncommitted sex [a hookup involving penetrative sex] reported a history of experiencing regret following such an encounter.[14]

The appeal of hooking up may be stronger than the actual results of the

---

Share This

It is not surprising when we look at the large number of young adults hooking up, since we are wired for that type of intimacy.

#everyonelovessex

---

act. Physical needs do get met, and one does not have to worry about relationship woes, but the real issue with hooking up seems to be people looking for something deeper—and from what the research and stories suggest, hooking up does not provide that. Since we are wired for relationships and hooking up does not seem to provide lasting fulfillment, many are still left empty.

Though it promises so much, it leaves a void. Alcohol is almost always used to get the encounter started. The concern with alcohol being involved is the question the next day of whether or not the hookup was consensual. It must be understood that "No" always means "No." However, alcohol and drug use also increase the chances of one partner being coerced into something that is not wanted.

The Justice Department surveyed 6,800 undergraduates at two large public universities and discovered that nearly 14 percent of the women (that is nearly 1,000 women!) indicated they had been victims of at least one sexual assault on campus. More than half of the victims indicated they were incapacitated from alcohol or drugs during the encounter.[15] Feeling as if one has been raped probably means that a rape did in fact take place, which is another indication that hooking up does not deliver. In trying to find a connection, something emotionally deeper through hooking up, what we see is that there is a danger of rape, emotional disconnection, and embarrassment. Just as they do with hooking up, people also turn to porn to find fulfillment and a sense of belonging.

Does Pornography Help Us Emotionally Connect?

In their search to find love, acceptance, and a sense of belonging, many people turn to a very unexpected place—pornography.

There is a reason there are over 500 million pages of pornography on the Internet, and that the pornography industry is a worldwide empire bringing in an estimated 97 billion dollars a year.[16] What is it about sex—and especially explicit sexual content on the Internet—that draws so many people? And a follow-up question might be this: Do they find what they are looking for?

This may come as a shock, but pornography is not about sex! In the same way that overeating is not really about food, but uses food as a vehicle for something deeper, so it is with pornography. In other words, there is something deeper that compels the food addict to eat excessively—and with pornography, there is something deeper that compels us to view it, sometimes even excessively. Pornography is

> **┌─ Share This ─┐**
> This may come
> as a shock, but
> pornography is
> not about sex!
> #everyonelovessex

about filling a need deep within us—a need to be loved, to belong, to feel worthy.[17] When those needs are not met, it is all too easy to turn to various alternative ways to meet those needs. Pornography promises so many things, but the haunting question is, does it really deliver what we long for and seek in it? If we were honest with ourselves, does pornography fulfill our needs for love, belonging, and worth?

Pornography offers so many promises. It can be easy to believe that God is not offering what is the very best for us, consequently leaving us to search for fulfillment from other sources. Author and counselor Michael John Cusick nearly threw his life away when he let his addiction to pornography progress into visiting strip clubs, hiring prostitutes, and lying to his wife. His is an amazing story of God turning a life around. In his book *Surfing for God: Discovering the Divine*

Desire Beneath Sexual Struggle, Cusick writes about what pornography promises but in actuality does not—and could never—deliver.

Porn and Marriage

Researchers wanted to study the effects pornography has on romantic relationships. In order to do this, researchers performed five separate studies. Here's what they discovered:

- The first three studies demonstrate that pornography consumption is related to weakened commitment to a romantic partner.
- Study four demonstrates that the more pornography one watches, the more likely one is to look into a different relationship.
- The fifth and final study showed an association between pornography consumption and being physically unfaithful to one's partner.[18]

First, pornography promises sexual fulfillment without relationship. Pornography separates the intimacy, closeness, and bond that is created with a spouse and offers only simulation. There is no relationship. There is no discussion of a future together. Moreover, it paints a picture of other human beings as mere objects to be used for pleasure. Any married couple will tell you that fulfilling sexual relations happen in the context of a healthy emotional relationship. Pornography promises just the opposite.[19]

Second, pornography promises intimacy without requiring risk and suffering. One of the scariest things I have ever done was propose to my wife, Caz. While I knew she would say "Yes!" I still feared putting myself out there because there was always the possibility of rejection. Looking back on our wedding day, the vows we repeated to each other have grown more real. At first, we did not know the full expression and ramifications of what we were promising to each other—but as time has passed, we have seen what it means to live out those vows. In the years we have been married, we have experienced so many different emotions: love, joy, hurt, pain, sadness, and so on. We both took a risk that Friday night in June 2010—a risk we were not fully awakened to. But now? We realize what those vows mean, what commitment and love mean—through the good and the bad. The risk—the intimacy—was worth everything. Pornography will have you believe that intimacy comes through a click, but nothing could be further from the truth.[20]

Third, pornography promises passion and life without connection to your soul. The lure of pornography is strong, promising an exciting, passion-filled experience. The problem is that it does nothing for the soul, other than smother it. There's no real life, no abundant life (John 10:10) that comes with pornography. Pornography only brings destruction. Pornography breaks down marriage vows, desensitizes us, and gives a false representation of love. Instead of pornography bringing a couple together or helping a single person in his or her relationships, it brings disconnection and destruction.

While pornography promises much, it sadly delivers very little in the end. There is no emotional connection, an essential need we have as human beings. And without that emotional connection to someone, sex is actually *much less* than what it can be. It becomes an act about gratification—and sadly, often at the expense of objectifying the other person. A healthy emotionally connected relationship involves trust, vulnerability, commitment, and empathy—all of the characteristics one needs to share life with someone. Pornography does not offer any of these characteristics—none. Trying to gratify yourself with sexual images does not equal intimacy or a healthy, emotionally connected relationship. It is a "solution" that can never be fulfilling.[21]

Did You Know?

1. The most expensive pornographic film made was in 2005, and it cost a little over 1 million dollars.
2. Between 25 percent and 35 percent of people who watch Internet porn are women.
3. In the United States there is a new pornographic video created every 39 minutes.
4. Professional porn actors are 80 percent less likely to get an STD than members of the public of the same age.
5. Approximately 12 percent of all websites have pornographic material.
6. Female porn actresses get paid an average of $600–$1,000 per scene. Men get paid less than $150.
7. Pornography makes up 30 percent of all data transferred across the net. At its peak, pornographic sites transfer 100 gigabytes of data per second.
8. Producing and distributing pornography can be punishable by death in countries like North Korea and Iran.
9. Some 20 percent of men admit to viewing pornography at work.
10. Every second an estimated 30,000 people are watching pornography.[22]

Men and women get hooked on pornography because of an emotional disconnection.[23] What we are really looking for is a healthy connection with another human being. Sadly, when we do not find it or are having relationship problems, the computer or phone is one of the first places we turn. We are wired for relationships, to feel like we are worthy. The reality is that if we turn to pornography to find that connection, we will always be left wanting, searching, longing for something more real than images on a screen.[24]

Brooklyn Finds Love, Fulfillment, Redemption, and a Sense of Belonging

Brooklyn had hit rock bottom. She was volunteering at a youth group, living with and having sex with guys—and had just had an abortion due to a pregnancy. There had to be more to life than just this. She picked up two books that would eventually change her life, *Crazy Love* and *When God Writes Your Love Story*. While reading these books, she began to experience some healing. For the first time in her life, she felt a sense of joy and peace that she had never felt before.

"I felt the overflowing of God's unfailing love! I realized that I no longer had to fill my emptiness with guys; I have someone more sustaining—more life-giving."

For the first time, Brooklyn understood what it meant to be embraced by the love of Jesus—and for the first time, she was truly able to receive that embrace. "I felt God's grace and compassion. And it just felt so good."

Brooklyn wanted to continue on this road to healing and redemption, so she made a bold first step—she left the world she was surrounded by. She started over, found new friends, sought

> **Share This**
> "I felt the overflowing of God's unfailing love! I realized that I no longer had to fill my emptiness with guys; I have someone more sustaining— more life-giving."
> #everyonelovessex

counseling, and really wanted to follow this Jesus she had experienced so strongly. She understood the importance of sexual faithfulness and wanted to be faithful to her future spouse from that moment on. She also came to a new understanding that these sexual relationships would never—and could never—fill the void that once dominated her life. She realized that these sexual experiences would never make her feel worthy or valuable.

I asked Brooklyn about redemption. She simply said, "I have confidence in the Lord that I am redeemed, that I am forgiven! And I am in the best place of my life." Brooklyn, now twenty-five, knows the value and importance of sexual faithfulness. Stepping into this new reality, she now spends time communicating this message to her friends, at churches, or at universities. Now that she has experienced both sides, she is on a mission to help bring healing to those who are willing to embrace it—and be embraced by it. And for the first time in her life, Brooklyn has been single for nearly a year and is extremely proud that she is learning to find her worth and identity in God.

One of the most powerful moments in my conversation with Brooklyn was when she told me that this past summer she called Jackson, the boy who had molested her in the sixth grade, and said, "I have forgiven you." To her surprise, he was quite vulnerable, telling her that he had been molested as a child. He knew the pain, and he was extremely sorry for what happened that night. Brooklyn truly has experienced redemption and now is living a life of freedom. The great news is that anyone, no

> **Share This**
> And because of Jesus' grace and redemption, it means we are worth it!
> #everyonelovessex

matter who they are or what they have been through, can experience this same redemption and freedom. And because of Jesus' grace and redemption, it means we are worth it!

You Are Worth It!

You have a place to belong and to be loved! That is what Brooklyn finally discovered. She didn't receive love or a sense of belonging from her mom (and her dad was not in the picture). But after trying everything else—things she thought would fulfill her—she realized that ultimate fulfillment only comes when the creation connects with the Creator.

I picture Brooklyn as the prodigal daughter in Luke 15. She left, trying to find a place to belong, trying to find fulfillment, trying to find meaning and joy—but she came up empty and alone. And the entire time her heavenly Father was just waiting for her to come back—because she is worth it.

There is a better way. There is a more fulfilling way. It is when we trust and live for our Creator that we find who we are—and learn that we are indeed worth it. We need to stop searching for meaning and belonging and love in places where we will never be fulfilled. Rather, we need to look to and live for the one who created us. He loves you! You are worth it!

CONTINUING THE DISCUSSION

1. Do you ever struggle with feeling you are valuable—that you are worth it? Why or why not?

2. Could you relate with Brooklyn's story?

3. What does every person need?

4. Are hookups the best way to find love and belonging?

5. Why can hookups be dangerous?

6. What real life story in this chapter impacted you the most? Why?

7. Do you believe pornography can help you emotionally connect to another person?

Have you shared your thoughts online yet?
#EveryoneLovesSex

Notes

[1]"What Is Sociology?" UNC Department of Sociology, http://sociology.unc.edu/undergraduate-program/sociology-major/what-is-sociology/.

[2]See Abraham Maslow's book *A Theory of Human Motivation.*

[3]Kate Taylor in the *New York Times* quotes Elizabeth A. Armstrong, a sociologist at the University of Michigan, who studies women's sexuality. "Sex on Campus: She Can Play that Game, Too," *New York Times*, July 12, 2013, http://www.nytimes.com/2013/07/14/fashion/sex-on-campus-she-can-play-that-game-too.html?pagewanted=all&_r=0.

[4]Ibid.

[5]Justin Garcia, Chris Reiber, Sean G. Massey, and Ann M. Merriwether, "Sexual Hookup Culture: A Review," *Review of General Psychology* 16.2 (2012): 163.

[6]A study by psychologists Jean Tweng and Brook Wells in Steven E. Rhoads, Laura Webber, and Diana Van Vleet, "The Emotional Costs of Hooking Up," *The Chronicle of Higher Education*, June 20, 2010, http://www.chronicle.com/article/The-Emotional-Costs-of-Hooking/65960/.

[7]This story is adapted from Kate Taylor, "Sex on Campus," *New York Times.*

[8]Sharon Jayson, "More College 'Hookups,' but More Virgins, Too," *USA Today*, March 30, 2011, http://usatoday30.usatoday.com/news/health/wellness/dating/story/2011/03More-hookups-on-campuses-but-more-virgins-too/45556388/1.

[9]Ibid.

[10]Garcia et al., "Sexual Hookup Culture," 201.

[11]Jayson, "More College 'Hookups.'"

[12]Garcia et al., "Sexual Hookup Culture," 4.

[13]Ibid., 3.

[14]Ibid.

[15]Christopher P. Krebs, Christine H. Lindquist, Tara D. Warner, Bonnie S. Fisher, Sandra L. Martin, "The Campus Sexual Assault (CSA) Study," December 2007, Final report to the National Institute of Justice, https://www.ncjrs.gov/pdffiles1/nij/grants/221153.pdf.

[16]John Gottman and Nan Silver, *What Makes Love Last? How to Build Trust and Avoid Betrayal* (New York: Simon and Schuster, 2012), 62.

[17]Michael John Cusick, *Surfing for God: Discovering the Divine Desire Beneath Sexual Struggle* (Nashville: Thomas Nelson, 2012), 16–20.

[18]Ibid.

[19]Ibid.

[20]Ibid.

[21] Michael J. Formica, "Female Objectification and Emotional Availability: Understanding the Social Dynamics of Pornography Addiction," *Psychology Today*, August 22, 2008, https://www.psychologytoday.com/blog/enlightened-living/200808/female-objectification-and-emotional-availability.

[22] Kathleen Miles, "Ten Facts about Porn Industry: 'All Time 10s' Video Shows How Big the Adult Industry Is," *Huffington Post*, October 31, 2012, http://www.huffingtonpost.com/2012/10/29/ten-porn-industry-facts-all-time-10s-video_n_2039449.html.

[23] Formica, "Female Objectification and Emotional Availability."

[24] If you need help, a great resource is www.xxxchurch.com, which will encourage you and assist you in freeing yourself from porn addiction. On the site, you can also take a survey to see if you are a porn addict: http://www.xxxchurch.com/sex-addiction-test.

The Vision of Sexual Faithfulness

Knowing why we should wait for the gift of marriage is one thing. Doing something about it—having a vision for what your life could be—is another. This section will paint a picture of a fulfilling life. The life Jesus promises us in John chapter 10. Now, that does not mean it is an easy undertaking. It does mean, however, that God gives us direction, purpose, and calls us to action. He calls us to really take a deep look at ourselves and ponder why we do what we do. This section will also encourage and not condemn you, wherever you are in your sexual journey. The goal is that once you know why you do what you do, you will be empowered to change. And when change starts with us, we allow God to work powerfully in our lives—resulting in us being a blessing to others. This section will also look at the difference between sex and love and why many confuse the two. Again, once you understand why you cannot feel love or receive love, it is then that change can happen.

After reading this section you will be equipped to change—equipped and empowered to find fulfillment. And it is possible. We serve a God who does not leave us broken, but who wants to mend us and redeem us. Once we receive that healing, we understand that sex and marriage are truly gifts from him. No longer will we feel that sex is bad or harmful—but we will realize sex is a gift. Read this section with an open heart, and ask God to help you cast the vision of sexual faithfulness for your life!

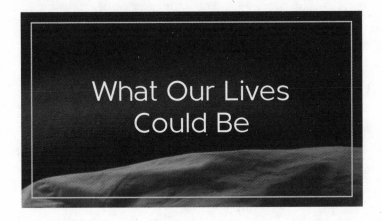

CHAPTER 4

What Our Lives Could Be

As someone who has a blog, I am always fascinated by how certain posts will get shared hundreds or thousands of times while others will go relatively overlooked. I recently posted a simple question on social media—and the response was more than I ever imagined. The question was this: *What do human beings need?* The responses ranged from "facials" to "religion." As I began to look deeper, however, something remarkable began to emerge. Two responses, in various forms, kept appearing over and over again. Two responses that affirm what many psychological, sociological, and relationship experts have been saying for decades. We have a deeply felt need to be *loved* and to be in *community*.

Would you agree with that? Do you feel this need to be loved and to belong?

> **Share This**
> Do you feel this need to be loved and to belong?
> #everyonelovessex

What would your life be like if you deeply experienced the love of God and others? What would your life be like if you felt a part of a community—and not only a sense that you belonged, but also that your presence was valued? What if your presence really mattered? How would all this change you?

What if I told you that this vision is exactly what God desires for each of us? You might say that it is too good to be true. You might look around and choose not to believe it. You might even think: *What about the world we live in? There is no way this is even possible.* Before we go any further, take a moment and ponder this question: *If you could have any kind of life you wanted, what would it look like?* Take just a minute to write down how you would answer that question. You might draw a picture or create a list of words. It might be a paragraph or even a Venn diagram. The important thing is to collect your thoughts about the *future*. This is not time to rehash the past—the past cannot be changed, but your *future* can. Dream—dream big.

I have asked this question before, and what I hear most is a life resembling something like this:

- Someone to fall in love with, someone whom you can trust and be yourself with
- Someone in your life who accepts you for who you are
- A job or career that brings fulfillment
- Being able to express yourself
- A successful life
- A loving family
- Healing from past wounds
- The ability to enjoy life and find fulfillment

Here is the beauty of the kind of life you described—you can actually have it! This is one of the amazing aspects of God. God wants us to have a fulfilled life. He wants us to enjoy life to the fullest. He has placed within us dreams and visions of what our lives could be—and how he can use us to impact his kingdom here on earth. He gives us the ability to choose him and the freedom to make our own decisions. But often the reality is that we stray, going after our own desires, lusts, and hopes, leaving God's design for us out of the equation. We use our freedom to choose what we think will bring us happiness, and when it does not, we begin to doubt that we could ever have a thriving and fulfilled life. But that is exactly what God wants for us! Could the decision *still* be ours to make?

All along God has given us so much. What he is asking us to do is to respond. He is pleading with us to not compromise our values, to not move in directions that are contrary to what will bring us lasting happiness. He is telling us over and over that when we move counter to how we are designed, we are settling—in our lives, in our relationships, and in the future.

As you painted the picture of your future, you may have even thought: *That would be nice, but it's not realistic!* Really!

Not realistic? Consider this. Isn't the one who created the universe and who lives within and empowers every believer the very same one who wants us to live a fulfilled life? Isn't the Jesus who said that he has come to give us life to the fullest (John 10:10) the same one who died and rose again in order to offer us a way to have that life? The Creator, who has redeemed us, is the very same one who has opened a way for us—empowering us to live life to the fullest.

Moreover, this is the same God who is good and sees that you are worthy of a full and rich life. Now, we are not worthy because of our actions. We are worthy because of Jesus' actions. So just try this for me as you read this chapter. Try to believe that God is good and that he has not forgotten you. In fact, he wants to be a part of your life! As you continue to read, process that thought—and let's start with the end in mind, namely how you want your life to be and what it will take to get there.

God is our Creator, sustainer, and one that gives us each breath we breathe. He created us in his image—to be his representation in this world. From the very beginning, God gave humanity the ability to experience life and relationships. He created feelings, intimacy, and yes—even our sexuality. Sexuality is a gift from God to each and every one of us.

Sexual faithfulness is much more than mere dos and don'ts. Sexual faithfulness is about living in harmony with how the Creator designed us. It is about living faithfully into the beauty and fullness of our sexuality—not about keeping a list of laws and regulations. Where did we get this notion of God's boundaries being a list of rules and laws?

> **Share This**
>
> Moreover, this is the same God who is good and sees that you are worthy of a full and rich life.
>
> #everyonelovessex

If one were to read the entire Old Testament and count all of the laws, we could come up with 613 laws that God gave the Israelites. But here's where it gets tricky. *Why* did God give them these laws? How we answer this question has everything to do with how we view God and our relationship with him. Did he give them these laws in order for them to earn his favor? Did he give them these laws so that they would have a relationship with him? The answer to these two questions is a surprising no.

God gave the Israelites these laws *after* they were chosen by his grace and said yes in response. In other words, the Israelites were already in a relationship with God when he gave them the Law. The Law was not about earning or striving. It was not a burden upon the people, but was a joy and a blessing (Ps. 119:97–104)! In giving the Law, God was offering the Israelites a way to live into the fullness of the relationship they already had with him.

Think of it like a marriage. A husband and wife do not live a certain way in order to prove they should get married. They do not have a long list of rules and laws they need to follow so they can get married. It's the exact opposite. A husband and wife live a certain way because they are married—to live into the fullness of what it means to be married. The boundaries are there not to prove you are married or to show whether you should get married. The boundaries in marriage are there for you to experience all that marriage is—to experience the best possible married life.

This is what the Law was meant to do—to show us how to live with God to the fullest.

Fast-forward to the New Testament. In Matthew 5–7—what we call the Sermon on the Mount—Jesus referred to a number of Old Testament laws, saying things like, "You have heard it was said, but now I tell you . . ." What is Jesus doing? Is he saying that the Law was bad? Is he changing the Law? Actually, Jesus is critiquing something larger than the Law. Rather than diminishing the Law, he is actually calling people to a higher way of living the Law. He is calling people back to the heart of the Law—a way of living into a full and right relationship with God. In fact, Jesus stated as much, saying, "Do not think that I have come to abolish the Law or the Prophets; I have not come to abolish them but to fulfill them" (Matt. 5:17). Jesus was calling people back to the real purpose of the Law. To understand all this, let's take a look at a common law that is still well known today.

The fourth commandment is to "Remember the Sabbath day by keeping it holy" (Exod. 20:8). The word *holy* means "set apart" for a sacred purpose, so the call here is to set aside the seventh day, the Sabbath (technically Saturday), for a sacred purpose—to rest and celebrate God. In order to make sure the people of God obeyed this law, other laws were added to ensure they kept the Sabbath holy. Why would they do this? Because Exodus 20:8 never explicitly explained *how* to keep the Sabbath holy. It was because of their desire to keep the original law that additional laws were added. In the Mishnah (Jewish oral traditions written down after the time of Jesus) there are in fact thirty-nine points, and even more subpoints, detailing what observant Jews can and cannot do on the Sabbath.[1] Some of them include no tying or untying of sandals, doing laundry, plucking out gray hairs, and saving your ox if it happens to be drowning in a ditch. We would look at these laws and see them as legalistic, but what if they are there as a way of protecting the people—guiding them into the heart and essence of the Law? What if instead of being a burden, they were actually a gift?

Jesus, far from abolishing the Law, came to fulfill it—to help people live it more faithfully. Jesus' critique was not about the laws themselves, but that people had lost sight of the heart of the Law—the way of living in connection with God—and instead found pride in "keeping the rules." This is why Jesus states, "For I tell you that unless your righteousness surpasses that of the Pharisees and the teachers of the law, you will certainly not enter the kingdom of heaven" (Matt. 5:20). Jesus was calling the people to radically return to their first love—God—and the passionate pursuit of living into the fullness of their connection with him.

Rather than seeing sexual faithfulness as a bunch of rules—dos and don'ts—what if we embraced them like the Jews, and Jesus and Paul, embraced the Law? What if rather than burdensome legalism, sexual faithfulness was a gift—a way to live into the fullness of all God desires for us sexually? I wonder what Jesus' critique would be of the church today in the way we often approach sexuality . . .

Is God Good?

The story of the Garden in Genesis 3 is one of harmony and goodness, of relationship and trust. But something goes horribly wrong. Humanity doubts the goodness of God. *Does God really have our best interests in mind?* Believing that God is in fact holding out on them, Adam and Eve eat from the tree of the knowledge of good and

---

Share This

Rather than seeing sexual faithfulness as a bunch of rules—dos and don'ts—what if we embraced them like the Jews, and Jesus and Paul, embraced the Law?

#everyonelovessex

---

evil—and everything changes. But rather than merely being a story about what happened—*what if the story is also about what is happening*? In other words, why do we, like Adam and Eve, doubt that God has our best interests in mind? The reality is this: we serve a good God who wants what is best for us. And even when we turn from him, he is still waiting patiently for us to return.

Part of the problem in believing that God is good is our upbringing. In psychology, the concept of "attachment theory" shows that our view of God is directly related to our view of our primary caregivers. Simply put, if our primary caregivers were abusive, manipulative, absent, or negligent, this will influence how we view God. For some of us, this is where our struggle to see God as good lies. If so, in order to view God as good and to truly embrace his love, it would be wise to start with counseling to get healing from our past.[2]

The Bible is clear that God is good. With that premise, it follows that God wants what is best for us. He wants us to thrive and live as we were designed to live. He is not holding back on us. He is not ashamed of us. In fact, he wants us to thrive! But whether consciously or subconsciously, we often use our freedom to live as we want. When we go against our design, we set ourselves up for mediocrity, selfishness, and bondage. As we misuse our God-given freedom, we drift further from what our life could really be.

Freedom

When it came to eating, I never had to worry about putting boundaries on what I ate. I ate—and never gained a pound! I never understood why that was a big deal until I got married. I have gained forty pounds since 2010—the year I married Caz.

As I write this, I am in the process of watching my calories and am doing well in getting to my ideal weight. What I am discovering is that as I eat right, avoid high calories, high fat, high-sugar foods, and work out, I actually feel better. In the months since I have been getting on track, I have noticed a tremendous increase in my energy level— and my old clothes are starting to fit again.

> **Share This**
>
> When we go against our design, we set ourselves up for mediocrity, selfishness, and bondage. As we misuse our God-given freedom, we drift further from what our life could really be.
>
> #everyonelovessex

I suppose some would ask, "Why even bother with working out?" Eat what you want and enjoy life. But I have found that there is actual freedom when I am living a healthy life: freedom in feeling good, freedom in more energy, freedom in keeping up with my children, and freedom in knowing I am not poisoning my body as I used to.

The most common definition of freedom in our culture is doing what we want, whenever we want. But is this truly freedom? Let's play this out to its logical conclusion. My friend, Eric, once told me of his "freedom" to drink whenever he wanted. For ten years he drank, often hiding it from those he loved the most—his family, wife, and kids. His addiction started spilling over into his personal and professional life, to the point that he had to enter a ten-month rehab program. I remember him telling me all about his "freedom"—sadly, it ended up more like bondage.

Tim was a friend of mine in college. He hooked up with whomever he wanted, because he was "free" to do so. One night he even hooked up with multiple girls. Years after college, he confided in me, saying that he and his then-wife were having serious sexual issues in their marriage because of their past sexual experiences. Sadly, there are still things they cannot do together physically because of their past experiences. Was it truly "freedom"?

Don't misunderstand me. There is grace and freedom that comes from Jesus even when we stray from our design; however, if we think freedom is doing what we want, whenever we want—we might want to reconsider. Over the fifteen-plus years I have been working with students, I have heard hundreds upon hundreds of people tell me that their sexual experiences before marriage were not worth it. The reason they often give for having had premarital sex centers on freedom—the oasis of freedom that sex before marriage offered turned out to be nothing more than a mirage.

Biblical Freedom

The kind of freedom that God has designed for all of us is starkly different from what our culture sees as freedom. Let's go back to the Garden of Eden. We read in Genesis, "You are *free* to eat from any tree in the garden; but you must not eat from the tree of the knowledge of good and evil" (Gen. 2:16–17, emphasis added). The first words of freedom spoken were at the Garden of Eden—but how could freedom and constraint go hand in hand? How can even a hint of restriction be true freedom? Notice God said you are free to eat whatever you want. That is exactly freedom in terms of how our culture views it. But then God

> **Share This**
> The first words of freedom spoken were at the Garden of Eden—but how could freedom and constraint go hand in hand?
> #everyonelovessex

adds a restriction—except for the tree of the knowledge of good and evil. Now, that is beginning to sound less like freedom and more like control.

Following this account to its logical conclusion, we see that Adam and Eve went against the freedom they were given. They felt God was holding something back from them; maybe they even felt there should be no limitations. So they ate—and the result? *Shame. Embarrassment. Insecurities. Alienation.*

Then when God came on the scene, they hid and blamed each other. Adam even blamed God. Again, this does not sound like freedom to me. As we process this idea of freedom as our culture has defined it and inculcated in us, hopefully we are coming to a deep realization that this type of "freedom" is not really freedom at all. In fact, from the very beginning, the story we think of as one that illustrates freedom is actually the very opposite. Roger Olson captures this beautifully when he observes, "It's a story of shame, hiding, alienation, enmity, toil, and death—in short, the absolute antithesis of freedom."[3]

The reality is that we have a choice to make. On the one hand, we can follow our culture's definition of freedom, doing what we want whenever we want. On the other hand, we can choose to follow God's design for freedom, believing he is good and has our best interests in mind. Adam and Eve chose the former and changed everything.

Jesus once stated, "So if the Son sets you free, you will be free indeed" (John 8:36). Jesus' message was clear: your old way of life is bringing you into bondage—but when you follow me and submit to me, you will experience freedom like you never have before!

Paul, someone who experienced this kind of freedom, powerfully echoed Jesus' words in Romans 8:1–4, proclaiming:

Therefore, there is now no condemnation for those
who are in Christ Jesus, because through Christ
Jesus the law of the Spirit who gives life has set you
free from the law of sin and death. For what the law
was powerless to do because it was weakened by the
flesh, God did by sending his own Son in the like-
ness of sinful flesh to be a sin offering. And so he
condemned sin in the flesh, in order that the right-
eous requirement of the law might be fully met
in us, who do not live according to the flesh but
according to the Spirit.

In the fourth century AD, Saint Augustine taught that freedom
was what we were created for, noting that true freedom only
comes when we conform to the image of God—Jesus Christ.
"The farther we drift from it [that is, who we were created to
be], the more our freedom shrinks."[4]

Olson, commenting on the fact that Adam and Eve had
paradise—and they threw it away for bondage, because of their
selfishness—makes this insightful comment:

The implication of the Genesis story is unavoidable:
True freedom is found only in obedience to God
and the fellowship that comes with it. Loss of true
freedom comes with self-assertion, the idolatrous
desire to rule my own square inch of hell rather
than enjoy the blessings of God's favor . . . This
gospel theme of true freedom through obedience
and servanthood is so pervasive in the Bible that it
cannot be missed. And yet, because of our culture's
overriding emphasis on autonomy, we miss it all
the time.[5]

If you really want to live a fulfilled life, like the one you created at the beginning of the chapter, the only way to do that is through obedience to God. He is the Creator and we are his creation. When we obey and submit to God, we are living free and fulfilled lives—because that is how we were designed to live. This is not say that the going will not be tough. It is not to say that we will not struggle. Freedom can lead to difficult choices. It is here that we need to remember what Jesus said to the people of his day:

> ┌─ **Share This** ─┐
> If you really want to live a fulfilled life, like the one you created at the beginning of the chapter, the only way to do that is through obedience to God.
> └─ #everyonelovessex ─┘

> Come to me, all you who are weary and burdened, and I will give you rest. Take my yoke upon you and learn from me, for I am gentle and humble in heart, and you will find rest for your souls. For my yoke is easy and my burden is light. (Matt. 11:28–30)

When we choose to live in the way God has designed us, we experience freedom—true freedom. God does not provide boundaries to be a burden, but to be a gift. The boundaries are not there to hinder our freedom, but to enhance it—even to help us experience it more deeply. The choice is ours. Do we want to embrace what our culture says is freedom, but is really nothing more than bondage? Or do we want to embrace the freedom that our Creator offers us, one that leads to a life fully free, fully fulfilled?

If you choose the latter, here is what your life could be:

- Your life could be one of excitement and fulfillment.
- Your life could be one where you do not have to settle.

- Your life could be one where you do not have to be the status quo.
- Your life could be one where you constantly discover how much you are loved.
- Your life could be one where, even though you have past hurts, you can find healing.
- Your life could be one free of anxiety, filled with peace.
- Your life could be one where you decide to make the right decisions from this point forward.

However, the only way your life can be like that is if you are truly free. Jesus has set us free from the bondage of sin—but it is up to us to live in that freedom. So what does that look like?

Living in freedom means we strive to honor God, not because we have to but because we want to respond to his love. It means we honor God by growing deeper in our relationship with him—seeking him on a more personal level. As we draw intimately closer to our Creator—our first love—we will naturally be aware of what honors him. The more we honor God—out of our natural response to his love—the more free and more fulfilled we will be. When we exercise freedom, we are setting ourselves up to live life to the fullest because we are living as we are designed to live.

Steps Forward

Go back to the vision of the kind of life you want in the future, one that you drew or wrote about at the beginning of the chapter. Now take a moment and write down a few steps you need to take to get there.

CONTINUING THE DISCUSSION

1. Is your life what you want it to be? If not, what needs to change? If so, why and how?

2. How do you define *community*?

3. Do you view sexual faithfulness as a gift from God?

4. Do you believe God is good and wants what is best for you?

5. How do you define *freedom*? How does this chapter define freedom from God's perspective?

6. In the beginning and end of this chapter, you had an opportunity to write or draw what you want your life to look like. How will you make that happen?

Have you shared your thoughts online yet?
#EveryoneLovesSex

Notes

[1] Ronald L. Eisenberg, "Shabbat's Work Prohibition," reprinted from *The JPS Guide to Jewish Traditions,* http://www.myjewishlearning.com/article /shabbats-work-prohibition/.

[2] You can go to www.aacc.net to find a list of quality Christian counselors.

[3] Roger Olson, the Foy Valentine Professor of Christian Theology and Ethics at Truett Theological Seminary of Baylor University, writes in an October 5, 2012, *Christianity Today* article, http://www.christianitytoday .com/ct/2012/october/bonds-of-freedom.html.

[4] Ibid.

[5] Ibid.

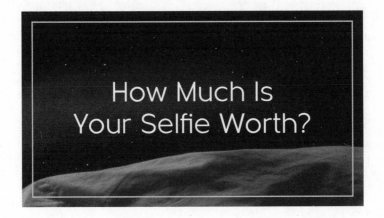

CHAPTER 5

How Much Is Your Selfie Worth?

Who hasn't taken a selfie? Whether showing off a new outfit or out eating with friends, we all take them. Kim Kardashian even has rules on how to take the perfect selfie. Our selfie must portray exactly what we want it to portray and be just right in order to get the most likes—which often translates into, "Therefore *I* must be liked."

The day I realized the selfie had taken the world by storm was a few years ago when I was on a house-building mission trip with Amor Ministries.[1] While working on the house we had been assigned to, I looked over and saw a group of students holding a selfie stick, taking multiple pictures to get the best shot. It was a surreal moment. On one hand, it was amusing, yet on the other hand, we were building a house for a family who could not afford a house. I wondered what the family thought. Our students, it seemed, were consumed with their selfie, not realizing the optics of the moment.

The Pope Takes Selfies!

On August 28, 2013, the same week that the word "selfie" officially made it into the *Oxford Dictionary*, a group of young people on a pilgrimage took a selfie with Pope Francis. This selfie has been officially deemed the first "Papal Selfie."[2]

If you think about it, selfies are a way of portraying what we want others to see—and we will take as many pictures as we need in order to get the picture that is just right. What's interesting about selfies is that we never see selfies of people when they are *not* looking their best. For example, I have yet to see the selfie of someone who captioned it "Just got fired!" I still haven't seen the selfie with the duck face and the caption "Don't you love my bad hair day?" I would love to see the selfie of a couple after a long argument with tears in the eyes that read, "I guess we don't have the perfect relationship! ☹"

It seems that all we see are selfies of the good times—or at least the *perception* of good times. And that is really one of the unspoken components of social media—we post the image of who we want to portray to the world. We are in charge of our image. What is inherent behind the selfie is a deep desire to be accepted, valued, respected,

> **Share This**
>
> We are in charge of our image. What is inherent behind the selfie is a deep desire to be accepted, valued, respected, and loved–the desires that are at the core of who we are as human beings.
>
> #everyonelovessex

and loved—the desires that are at the core of who we are as human beings. In other words, the desire is a common thread in the fabric of what it means to be human. Yet how we go about fulfilling those needs has everything to do with whether we will truly feel accepted, valued, respected, and loved.

There is a real danger in trying to fulfill those needs through social media. Because the reality is that the number of followers, likes, and shares we have has nothing to do with who we are as a person. When we rely on social media to dictate our value, we unwittingly give social media power over our image of ourselves. In other words, if our Instagram post does not get likes, we begin to question: Why? How we answer that simple question says a lot about the amount of power we give social media over our image of ourselves. The Bible presents a counternarrative, one where we are loved unconditionally and because of who we are—even when no one is looking (or "liking"). Jesus embodied this counternarrative—seeing value in everyone regardless of status, gender, or nationality. In the process, he called people into a new community—a new family—where we could learn from one another, encourage one another, and love one another.

Let me put it this way: So how much is your selfie worth? Is it worth basing our image on our likes, shares, or retweets? Do we really get the acceptance we *think* we get? Is the number of likes we receive really tied to who we are—or to the "image" we portray? *What if we felt the freedom to be who we truly are?* What if we felt free from the burden of what other people think about us?

> **Share This**
>
> The price of your selfies is what you are willing to sacrifice for real authentic community.
>
> #everyonelovessex

How might this change our lives? What kind of community would we experience?

The price of your selfies is what you are willing to sacrifice for real authentic community. Are you willing to trade likes for community? Are you willing to trade shares or retweets for honest feedback? What are you willing to put in lieu of community? How much is your selfie really worth?

The Television Show That Is the Epitome of Community

One of my favorite shows from the 1990s and early 2000s is *Friends*. It had an all-star cast: Jennifer Aniston, Matthew Perry, Courteney Cox, Matt LeBlanc, Lisa Kudrow, and David Schwimmer. Even though this show is not up to date with current affairs and technology, people still flock to watch it on Netflix. While it has been over a decade since the series finale, *Friends* still draws a weekly audience of 16 million views in the United States—and that does not include streaming. Even at Warner Bros. Studio in Burbank, California, where you can go on a tour of the set, it is not uncommon for proposals to happen on the very couch at Central Perk. Netflix caught on to this ever-expanding popularity and paid an estimated $118 million for the rights to stream it.[3]

But what is it about this show that continues to connect with people? This is a show that started in 1994 when everyone was getting email for the first time and ended in 2004 when people started signing up for Facebook. "Part of the appeal is wish-fulfillment," says co-creator Marta Kauffman, who adds that "because they're on social media all the time . . . I believe they crave human contact. They crave intimacy, and intimate relationships."[4]

A Millennial's Take on *Friends*

On *Friends*, "in their free time, they all get together in the coffee shop to chat and catch up," says Stephanie Piko, a twenty-one-year-old fan of the show. "Where nowadays we'll catch up really quickly, but everyone's always on their phones. Back then, it's more of a person-to-person relationship, instead of through technology." In hindsight, that era seems idyllic by comparison: a fantasy life where friends gather on a sofa, not on WhatsApp.[5]

Everyone craves intimacy and connection—to be known and to know another. There is something innate within each of us that longs for that kind of relationship, to have a group of people who know the real you—and still love you nonetheless. This type of intimacy comes through community—real community—one in which there is safety and freedom in sharing our fears, desires, and the future. It's the very thing I think Jesus had in mind for all his followers to experience. In fact, I would say community is essential to the Christian life.

A New Community

As we read through the Bible, it is evident that community is essential to being a part of the family of God. Meals, prayers, drawing water—all were done in community. You associated with others like you; you ate with others like you. That was what you did. However, when people started to follow the way of Jesus, this new rabbi, they were doing more than merely adding new teachings to their lives—they were entering a *new* community. This was a community that loved one another, cared for one another, supported one another. They met each other's needs, even took the burdens of others on themselves as their own. It was a new way of life—a new way of seeing themselves, the world, and those around them. Following the way of Jesus changed everything.

What we see in the early days of the Jesus movement is a deep commitment to one another; in other words, community. This was a community that not only embraced Jews but every nationality, status, and gender. Women were highly valued in the Jesus movement, even given places of leadership. It was a community that truly became family. There was trust, vulnerability, openness, and authenticity. They shared everything they had—and enjoyed being together. It was this new sense of family that caused the rapid growth of the movement.

In biblical times, people would only have dinner with those who shared common values and theological beliefs—and even more so if you were a religious leader. On a number of occasions Jesus was criticized for eating with "those types of people." The criticism was founded on the belief that if Jesus is eating with tax collectors (who were thieves) or people who made their income from selling their bodies, then he must agree with them—maybe even condone their actions.[6]

Where you sat or reclined at the dinner table also indicated your social standing. The closer you reclined to the host, the more highly respected you were. Conversely, the further away you reclined, the less honor you held within that community. Some people would even get to a meal early to try to claim a place near the host. Jesus once called out a group of people for doing just that:

> He went on to tell a story to the guests around the table. Noticing how each had tried to elbow into the place of honor, he said, "When someone invites you

to dinner, don't take the place of honor. Somebody more important than you might have been invited by the host. Then he'll come and call out in front of everybody, 'You're in the wrong place. The place of honor belongs to this man.' Red-faced, you'll have to make your way to the very last table, the only place left." (Luke 14:7–9 *The Message*)

The apostle Paul wrote the first recorded words of Jesus in 1 Corinthians.[7] He records what Jesus instructs his disciples regarding the Lord's Supper (1 Cor. 11:17–34). Shortly after Jesus' death, burial, resurrection, and ascension, the early church started meeting regularly for meals. These meals became known as *love feasts.*

At these love feasts, poor and rich, Jew and Gentile, men and women, the outcast and the dignified, would all gather together for a meal. In a society where honor and perception were extremely important, this was countercultural. Up until this point in ancient society, no one would have ever done anything like this. One commentator writes, "Within their own limits they had solved . . . the social problem which baffled Rome. They had lifted women to their rightful place, restored the dignity of labor, [and] abolished beggary."[8] They were able to do this because they believed that Jesus' sacrifice on the cross was the unifying act that brought all of humanity together. We are no longer aliens in a foreign

Share This

"Within their own limits they had solved . . . the social problem which baffled Rome. They had lifted women to their rightful place, restored the dignity of labor, [and] abolished beggary."

#everyonelovessex

land (Eph. 2), but rather brothers and sisters. His sacrifice made us a family—made us a community.

It would mean that on some days you might sit next to the wealthy, some next to the poor, some next to religious leaders, and others next to a prostitute. The common thread was that everyone realized they were sinners and that it was only because of Jesus that they were now a new family—not a superficial family, but one whose members cared about one another, cherished one another, and supported one another.

Over time, however, this meal started turning into something different from what Jesus intended. Instead of a place where all would share in Communion (the very representation of Jesus' unifying act), it started to become an exclusive club. Instead of waiting, the rich would enjoy their meal, and by the time others arrived, all they had left were their free samples and scraps. Then, in a mockery of the community Jesus initiated, they would take Communion as a way of saying that we are all brothers and sisters in Christ. The apostle Paul was so frustrated when he heard this report that he penned this rebuke:

> In the following directives I have no praise for you, for your meetings do more harm than good. In the first place, I hear that when you come together as a church, there are divisions among you, and to some extent I believe it. So then, when you come together, it is not the Lord's Supper you eat, for when you are eating, some of you go ahead with your own private suppers. As a result, one person remains hungry and another gets drunk. Don't you have homes to eat and drink in? Or do you despise the church of

God by humiliating those who have nothing?
(1 Cor. 11:17–18, 20–22)

The Lord's Supper was a time to live out the unifying nature of Christ; however, this did not always happen. Rather than it being a time to remember the gift of Christ and that we are a new community with new brothers and sisters, this meal became a meal of selfishness and self-interest.[9] Rather than it being a picture of community and living together into the way of Jesus, this meal showed division.

We All Want Community–Elaine's Story

I first met Elaine at the beginning of her senior year. She introduced herself to me and asked if we could chat. As she sat in my office, she was reserved and timid. Later, I would discover that she was not sure how I would respond to her struggles with doubts, substance abuse, and being in and out of rehab. From that first conversation to now as she prepares to graduate, I can say that I have never heard a more compelling story about community. I have never seen someone's eyes light up so much as when Elaine talks about what community means to her. Where did she find such an amazing community? I wish I could say it was the church, but it's Alcoholics Anonymous (AA)! In order to get the full grasp of her story, we need to start at the very beginning.

"At school, if there was that one uncool person that you didn't want to be associated with—that would have been me. I didn't have any school friends."

Elaine grew up in a middle-school youth group. She had one friend in the youth group and was close to the youth pastor and his wife. Other than that, she was a wallflower. It was

during this time that she was sexually abused by a neighbor—
an act she kept secret for many years.

At the age of twelve, Elaine developed an eating disorder as
a defense mechanism to the sexual abuse she experienced. She
lost thirty-four pounds over the next two years. At a summer
camp, tired of spinning out of control, she mustered up the
courage to tell her youth pastor about the abuse and her eating
disorder. After camp, and talking with her parents and her
doctor, she entered rehab for the first time. She was fourteen.

"Living with other girls who did not want to eat . . . you
bonded over that. But that community disappears when everyone leaves and goes back home . . ."

Almost a year later, Elaine continued her downward spiral
and went back to rehab for a second time. It was during this
second stint in rehab that she celebrated her second consecu-
tive birthday in treatment.

Things seemed to change after her second stint in rehab.
She started working and was doing independent study in order
to graduate high school on time. It was then that the drinking started.

She started with drinking her dad's alcohol at home, but
when that was not enough, she would have other people buy
it for her. Sometimes she would spend her whole paycheck
on alcohol.

She was on track to graduate early. She didn't go to parties,
so she thought her drinking was under control, but it wasn't.
She would drink every night in her room—alone. Sometimes
she would drink until she blacked out. She had no real friends,
no real community to speak of. She felt trapped and alone. As
the alcohol stopped being as effective at numbing her pain,
she began cutting herself—just to feel something. With the

drinking beginning to subside, her eating disorder came back with a vengeance.

One night, after binge drinking and excessive cutting, she blacked out on her floor and awoke the next day in a pool of blood. The medical examiner was surprised that she did not bleed to death overnight.

"I can still remember the night. I was really drunk—and had not blacked out yet. I just wanted to numb everything out, but nothing worked. The alcohol used to work. It used to numb the pain of the sexual abuse, but over time it stopped having that effect. I tried cutting, and after a time that was not working. I remember thinking, 'I have to let my mom know I have a problem. I can't stop.' Thankfully I sucked at killing myself."

The preliminary medical report noted that her cutting was so significant that she basically had skinned herself. She still has scars from that night.

It was her third time in rehab, only this time for a much shorter period, not because she was getting better, but because insurance stopped covering the expense. It was July, and she was about to begin college in a month. It was then that she got connected with AA.

She was given a counselor and a sponsor and began her steps to recovery. She started going to meetings— meetings she still goes to up until this day. Elaine just turned twenty.

---**Share This**---

The alcohol used to work. It used to numb the pain of the sexual abuse, but over time it stopped having that effect.

#everyonelovessex

AA as Community?

I have to admit something. Every time I would talk with Elaine, watching her eyes light up when she talked about community, I had to ask myself this question: Why isn't this kind of community everywhere—even in the church? I'll let Elaine explain it:

> In Alcoholic Anonymous we view alcoholism and addiction as a spiritual disease. So there's something fundamentally different about us, not different in *you're such a unique snowflake* way, but different as in our brains work a little bit differently.
>
> There's something about being able to go to anywhere in the world—and go to an AA meeting—and be fully at home. You know that people there understand your sickness on a deep spiritual level—you're messed up in the same way I am. They have been there as well. And there is something about sharing that with other people that is freeing.

The reality is this. In Elaine's time at church, she never experienced connection with someone on a deep spiritual level—in a way that they actually "got her."

> You can go to church and believe in the same Savior, but never have a connection on a deep spiritual level—and never be accepted for who you really are on the inside. In AA, they understand your sickness. They embrace you as you are. I feel that I am okay to be myself and do not have to worry about being judged.
>
> AA is about humbling yourself, being honest with yourself, and listening to other people. It is not about you. It is about other people. When I am recovering, I am getting better, and I become a better person by helping others.

There's something really special about going through your entire life as a mess-up or a reject of society and then finding people who actually care about you and love you and want to talk to you and have a relationship with you. It fosters a family atmosphere.

Even if I go into a meeting and I think some other person is a bigot, a jerk, or a hypocrite, we can both agree about our disease. And if it comes down to it, I know that he or she will have my back. They might hate my guts, but I know if I text them "I'm about to relapse," they will pick up the phone and be there. And it would be the same thing back and forth.

It's part of our responsibility as people who had this chance to get sober. You had this chance to get sober, and for some reason you stayed sober. For some reason you are alive today. God knows why. Now it is our job. It's part of the steps to carry this message and help other alcoholics. And part of that is answering the phone.

Now it would be easy for us to say that every church is just like that—*in theory*. Yet the reality is that far too often *in practice*, the church is anything but what Elaine just described. This may be a hard truth for those of us in the church to hear, but it's something we need to hear. Those who were broken and hurting flocked to Jesus. Today, often they want nothing to do with the church. Something is very wrong with this picture. For the churches that are "getting it," you are blessed—and are an encouragement to so many.

My First Time at an AA Meeting!

In June of 2016, Elaine invited an administrator and myself to her four-year celebration of sobriety at one of her AA meetings. We didn't know what to expect. As we drove down this dimly lit alleyway, we both wondered if we were in the right place. When we saw the pillar of cigarette smoke, we knew we had found it. Elaine met us in the parking lot, where about fifty others were gathered before the meeting. Inside the meeting, I came away with two highlights. One, there was no judgment in the group. Some talked about a relapse they experienced and others talked about how their journey was going strong. There was a sense that everyone was rooting for one another, regardless of how close they were relationally. Two, the group was attentive when those who were celebrating a sobriety milestone were sharing. I have never felt something that unique before. I finally got to experience the community Elaine's eyes would always light up about.

What I have found in my recovery community is love and acceptance and friendship. When speaking about the Christian church, I believe those are things God calls us to do—to love people, to accept other people, and to be in fellowship and community with other people. And I think that everyone in the world, not just Christians, needs to take a step back and evaluate ourselves first. It's the whole "be careful about the speck in your neighbor's eye when there is a log in your own."

I wonder. What if the church were more like the recovery community that Elaine knows so well? How might communities be changed? How might it change the reputation of "church" in our culture? Perhaps we would be known more for love than judgment, more for acceptance than rejection, and more for embrace and community. My hope and prayer is that we as the church will be known for our love, for our acceptance, and for our embrace. For when we are known for those kinds of things, the world will *know* that we are his disciples—for our love for one another.

We Are Made for Connection and Intimacy

From the very beginning verses of Genesis to the closing chapters of Revelation, we see one major theme throughout—the fact that we were made for connection and intimacy. The reason we long for community, deepness, and meaning is because that is how we are created, and we see this clearly in what Jesus instituted among his followers. As you reflect on the community Jesus invites us into, there may be something stirring within you. And the reason is quite simple: this is what *you* were created for. Sometimes it is easy to see this kind of connection as something for someone else—even something unattainable for us personally—but the fact of the matter is that this desire is hardwired in each of us and something we're each capable of. In this community everyone is welcomed, regardless of your status, what you have done, or how you view yourself. Yet at the same time, no matter how appealing this kind of community is, some fear it and try to fill the desire for connection and intimacy in other ways.

> **Share This**
> In this community everyone is welcomed, regardless of your status, what you have done, or how you view yourself.
> #everyonelovessex

Acknowledging that there is something missing, an emotional void, some will try to fill that need through sexual encounters—but because of the stories you have read here and possibly your own experiences or the experiences of your friends, you know the potential dangers. The question is then, why do we do it? Why do we try to fill that emptiness with anything other than what God has designed for us? Part of the reason is that we often "want the destination without the journey."[10] In other words, we know what we want, but either we don't know how to get there or we make choices that make getting to the destination more difficult—all because we want a quicker route. So think about this. What is the destination for you? Is it a committed relationship, loving partner, quality friendships, being mentally and emotionally healthy? What is it for you? Now the follow-up question is this: How do you get there? An even more telling question might be this: Is what I am doing right now helping or hurting my journey toward that destination? Moreover, what if we already have the ingredients for a healthy, godly community but have missed them because we have been too focused on sexual encounters—duping ourselves into believing that they will fill our need?

God created us for one another. It is in community where we are challenged, admonished, loved, cared for, nurtured, grow spiritually, and learn about ourselves. Community is being invited into someone's heart to see their dreams and fears as well as their doubts, secrets, and uncertainty with their future.[11] Community, true community, is that powerful!

Have you ever felt so safe in a community that you have shared your heart's desire for your life, shared your darkest moments? Have you ever felt a connection with others so deep that you know you can say whatever you want and not be judged? If you answered yes, then you know the richness and fulfillment that comes from what God has created us for. If you said no, take a moment and ponder if that could be one of the reasons you have searched for intimacy and connection through sexual encounters.

Living an Unfiltered Life

When we experience true community, we do not have to put on façades or project the image that we have everything together. In a healthy community, everyone has the right to get underneath the surface of what is going on. In other words, healthy communities look past the selfie image. When you get past the selfie, past the filters, you get to the real you—the unfiltered you. And it's when those filters are gone that we are left vulnerable, without any protection. This is why it is easy to choose to not be authentic and real and instead to find surface-level temporary comforts. When we are in true, healthy community, we can no longer hide behind the filters. Therefore, we need to stop pretending and start to get healing, forgiveness, wisdom, and love. Because we cannot fulfill our deepest, most essential human needs when we are pretending with the filters.

Here's the beauty of community—you have imperfect people coming together unfiltered—and because of their vulnerability, they leave stronger and more connected to Christ and one another. Healthy communities fill emptiness and voids that linger deep in our souls. They point us to Jesus.

Imagine if we felt the freedom to be who we truly are. What if we felt free from the burden of what other people

> **Share This**
> Healthy communities fill emptiness and voids that linger deep in our souls. They point us to Jesus.
> #everyonelovessex

think about us? These things happen in healthy community. For some, healthy communities seem like a pipe dream, something simply unattainable. If that's you, here are a few places to start on the journey toward community:

- Look at the people around you and see if you already have the potential of a healthy community—perhaps it has been there on the margins all along.
- Consider seeing a professional Christian counselor. Think of a counselor as a good friend who knows what they are talking about.
- Give yourself permission to be vulnerable. Usually when one opens up, it is easier for others to follow.
- Ask God to open your eyes in finding a healthy community.

What Your Life Could Be

Your life could be one in which your selfie is worth so much! In fact, it could be priceless if you do not settle. You are worth so much more than giving in to the social pressures of having to look a certain way, act a certain way, hook up a certain way. Nothing is worth more than your unfiltered self. You are a child of God, cherished by him. Validation, acceptance, popularity, whatever you are looking for is not found is sexual encounters or selfies. Rather, they are found in community.

Take a moment to reflect on your life. What do you like about your life now? What do you not like about your life? Are you fulfilled? Chances are, how you answer those questions will depend on whether or not you are in a healthy community. If you want to live a life where you are fulfilled, living for yourself will not bring fulfillment.

I have seen the stage production of *A Christmas Carol* close to ten times, as a neighbor is a local acting professional and has starred in the show every Christmas. The main character, Ebenezer Scrooge, is an unhappy tyrant of a business owner who keeps to himself, focusing on making money, because he has no need for community. Then one day he realized the world was more than making money—and he has an awakening.

> He went to church, and walked about the streets, and watched the people hurrying to and fro, and patted the children on the head, and questioned beggars, and looked down into the kitchens of houses, and up to the windows; and found that everything could yield him pleasure. He had never dreamed that any walk—that any thing—could give him so much happiness.[12]

A Christmas Carol paints the picture of someone as far away from living in community as possible. Ebenezer Scrooge stayed to himself, focused on making money and hoarding his belongings. He had no joy, no community, and no pleasure in life. But when Scrooge awakens to the meaning of life, he begins to live by another set of values, valuing the people around him. His life is transformed. He quite literally becomes a new person, a new creation. Pop culture, the early church, and now classic literature all seem to be tapping into the same truth—community is essential to a healthy life.

Share This

Pop culture, the early church, and now classic literature all seem to be tapping into the same truth—community is essential to a healthy life.

#everyonelovessex

And when you and I live in community, we experience fulfillment like we have never experienced before.[13]

Your life could be one that is fulfilled and full of pleasure because you are living in community with others. You can have a life where you wake up, knowing you are not perfect and your community is not perfect, but knowing that they are there for you through it all. You can live a life where you no longer have to search for fulfillment in sexual encounters—because you find fulfillment in healthy, unfiltered community.

Take a moment to write what you want your life to look like in regard to sexual faithfulness and community.

_____

_____

_____

_____

_____

_____

_____

_____

Finding Community–Domo's Story

True community can come in many different forms and can be found in many unexpected places. It can be found in a church, or even on a basketball court in mid-March.

Across the cafeteria table sat Domo, a six-foot-five muscular point guard from our men's basketball team. Domo has a smile that lights up a room—and a heart as big to match it. I met Domo two years ago when he transferred in to play basketball. Over those two years, we have had numerous meals and conversations together. I have also watched a countless number of his games and practices as a part of the men's basketball team. Seeing him in different settings, I have always been impressed by the level of respect he has for his peers and for the faculty and staff on campus. So, I wanted to ask about his thoughts on basketball, church, and community.

Over lunch, we started by talking about the journey of this year's season. We talked about early morning practices and running bleachers. "We had to rely on one another. If someone was lagging, we would pull and help him get through. We needed the support of one another. It was simple—we started this together, and we are going to finish it together."

There were times behind closed doors where they would argue, but they were always committed to working through the ups and downs. When the coach would get on a player, others would come alongside and offer him encouragement. If Domo or one of the other veteran players on the team felt the coach was too soft on a player, they would pull him aside and come down hard on him. "We were a team—a family. Everyone was committed to winning and supporting one another."

> The idea of community really hit me when we were playing in the GSAC [Golden State Athletic Conference] tournaments. You see all the fans coming to support the team, and you realize that this is bigger than one person, or even a team. Not only are there people there watching the game, but the game is nationally televised—so there's all kinds

of people watching the game. It was then that I realized that we were supported by more than just each
other; we were being supported by an entire college community.

We also talked about church and what kind of influence his
church community had on him growing up. "The community in my church was a shield. It helped me to stay focused
on God instead of drifting off. The church was my base of support; they were my extended family."

It was in his church community that he experienced support, love, and a sense of belonging.

Community has had a profound effect in my life.
There were many times when I could have taken a
negative turn or positive turn. I was always encouraged to see the bigger picture—the larger eternal
picture. You can see the negative effects on people
who lack community. You can see what they lack
because they resort to other things. They seek what
they are lacking in something else. And sadly, it
never works.

I look at where I am at today—I cannot take
the credit for myself. I have to give the credit to my
church community for where I am. They are the
ones who supported me. They are the ones who
looked out for me and loved me. They were the
ones who embraced me and helped me see what is
important in life. Without community, there is no
telling where I would be today.

CONTINUING THE DISCUSSION

1. With which famous person would you love to take a selfie?

2. When you post on social media, do you usually post the good stuff or the bad stuff?

3. Have you ever been disappointed when someone did not "like" a photo you posted, or when it did not get as many likes or shares as you had wanted?

4. Put the early church community narrative in your own words.

5. What was the most impactful part of Elaine's story?

6. Are you able to be honest and vulnerable in your community?

7. What does it mean that we are made for community and intimacy?

Have you shared your thoughts online yet?
#EveryoneLovesSex

Notes

[1] Check out what Amor Ministries is doing at www.amor.org. One of the reasons they focus on building homes is that it keeps families together, which means it keeps the human traffickers away.

[2] "A Brief History of the Selfie," *Huffington Post*, October 15, 2013, http://www.huffingtonpost.com/2013/10/15/selfie-history-infographic_n_4101645.html.

[3] Adam Sternbergh, "Is 'Friends' Still the Most Popular Show on TV? Why So Many 20-somethings Want to Stream a 20-year-old Sitcom About a Bunch of 20-somethings Sitting around in a Coffee Shop," *New York Magazine*, March 21, 2016, http://www.vulture.com/2016/03/20-somethings-streaming-friends-c-v-r.html.

[4] Ibid.

[5] Ibid.

[6] Jerome H. Neyrey, ed., *The Social World of Luke-Acts* (Peabody, MA: Hendrickson, 1991), 364.

[7] The Gospels were written after Paul's letters; consequently, the Lord's Supper, a sacred time where we remember the sacrifice of Jesus, is the first recorded words we have of Jesus.

[8] William Barclay, *The Letters of the Corinthians,* The Daily Study Bible Series, Rev. Ed. (Philadelphia: Westminster Press, 1975), 101–2.

[9] As Paul is correcting the Corinthians about the Lord's Supper, he writes in 1 Corinthians 11:27, "So then, whoever eats the bread or drinks the cup of the Lord in an unworthy manner will be guilty of sinning against the body and blood of the Lord." I have heard this passage used in a multitude of different ways. However, in this context everything is about community, therefore "in an unworthy manner" must refer to disunity. William Barclay writes, "This may mean that he who eats and drinks unworthily has never realized the whole Church is the body of Christ but is at variance with his brother. Every man in whose heart there is hatred, bitterness, contempt against his brother man, as he comes to the Table of our Lord, eats and drinks unworthily." See Barclay, *The Letters of the Corinthians,* 105.

[10] Phrase taken from Ashley Abramson, "4 Things Keeping Us from True Community: Building Real Community Takes Time, Emotion and Effort—Because That's What True Community Is All About" *Relevant Magazine*, June 9, 2015, http://www.relevantmagazine.com/life/4 -things-keeping-us-true-community.

[11] Gordon MacDonald, "True Community: What 'We' Learn That 'I' Will Never Know," *Christianity Today*, October 2014, http://www .christianitytoday.com/le/2014/october/true-community.html. Limited access.

[12] Charles Dickens, *A Christmas Carol* (London: Bradbury & Evans, 1858), 97.

[13] Jeremy Jernigan, *Redeeming Pleasure: How the Pursuit of Pleasure Mirrors Our Hunger for God* (Franklin, TN: Worthy, 2015), 193.

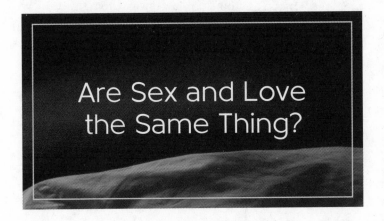

CHAPTER 6

Are Sex and Love the Same Thing?

Why Are Love and Sex So Powerful?

There's nothing quite like a good love story, right? These kinds of stories are compelling. They draw us in. The classic is Shakespeare's *Romeo and Juliet*. The story is set in Italy, where there is an ongoing feud between the Montague and Capulet families. Romeo and Juliet were two teenagers from opposing families who, against all odds and circumstances, fall in love and secretly marry.

Juliet, with the help of the friar who secretly married them, concocts a potion by which she would appear dead for two days. She figured if everyone thinks she's dead, after awakening, she can run off with Romeo and live happily ever after. Juliet was to drink the potion; then Romeo would come to her tomb where she lay and be there when she wakes. However, Romeo never got word of Juliet's plan, so when he heard of her apparent suicide, he was heartbroken. He ran to her tomb, saw her dead, and because he felt he couldn't live without her, killed himself. Juliet awoke from the two-day sleep, saw Romeo dead, and then killed herself.

This story has love, familial conflict, a secret marriage, and an unrelenting desire of two people in love—all of which speaks to our heart's desire to be loved. This story, written in the sixteenth century, is still studied today. One of the reasons is that the story is compelling. Everyone wants to find his or her Romeo (the man who will metaphorically kill to protect your love) or Juliet (someone so madly in love with you that there is no end to what she would do for you out of love).

> **Share This**
> Everyone wants to find his or her Romeo (the man who will metaphorically kill to protect your love) or Juliet (someone so madly in love with you that there is no end to what she would do for you out of love).
> #everyonelovessex

In the story, Romeo and Juliet consummate their marriage —but the story is not about their physical act of sex. It is about the longing these two have to be together—love. Sadly, today, for many people sex equals love—as if the physical act of sex will magically turn to feelings of love within both partners. But as we have seen—and will continue to see—that is truly a fairy tale.

Sex is literally the closest two people can ever be physically —but at the same time, it does not automatically produce intimacy. Intimacy comes when two people—two souls—open themselves up to be vulnerable and open to their partner on a deep, intimate level. This kind of connection is what we seek for in sex, thinking that we will somehow magically attain it during sex. Yet ironically, it is just the opposite—we are usually left unconnected, disjointed, and with a sense of loneliness and regret. Why? Because sex cannot give what we seek. In fact, it is intimacy and connection that two people share *outside* of sex that makes sex so intimately powerful. Without connection and intimacy outside of sex, there can never be connection and intimacy within sex.

What Is Love?

How we were raised and the types of relationships we have had, whether we want to admit it or recognize it, has implications for how we relate to others and to God. In fact, after a thirty-year longitudinal study (where scientists studied the same 1,377 people for a thirty-year period), scientists discovered that the number-one indicator of mental illness was how a person's primary caregiver, particularly one's father, treated them.[1]

All this to say that our past plays into our future, whether hurtful or healthy. It has even been said that our past is not our past—if we still let it affect our present. The sad fact is that many of us struggle with love and intimacy because of our upbringing. With this in mind, let's look at some possible reasons why it may be difficult for some people to receive and give love.

Before we get into a discussion of what love is, we need to spend some time exploring how we deal with relationships. This brings us closer to the heart of why some people can receive love, why some people run from it, and why others do not believe love even exists. My hope is that we might gain a

> **Share This**
> Without connection and intimacy *outside* of sex, there can never be connection and intimacy *within* sex.
> #everyonelovessex

glimpse of why we react to love the way we do—and how we can fully receive love.

In their book, *God Attachment: Why You Believe, Act, and Feel the Way You Do About God*, Tim Clinton and Joshua Straub write about four different relationship styles, how each is developed, and how to find healing from past wounds in order to experience a life that is free and healthy. The four relational styles or attachment styles are Secure Attachment, Anxious Attachment, Avoidant Attachment, and Fearful Attachment. We develop these relationship styles depending on how we answer two important questions. First, am I worthy of love? This is what we believe about our self-worth. Second, are others capable of loving me? This addresses our perception of whether or not others are trustworthy and reliable.[2] As we explore each of these relational attachment styles, perhaps you will see yourself in one or more of them. We will start with the emotionally and relationally healthy attachment style first—the one all of us want to be.

> **—Share This—**
> The four relational styles or attachment styles are Secure Attachment, Anxious Attachment, Avoidant Attachment, and Fearful Attachment.
> #everyonelovessex

Secure Attachment

Since I am a father of two daughters, every now and again I like to ask female students I feel are well-adjusted, respectful, and emotionally balanced about their upbringing. I am particularly interested in how I can be the best dad to my Abby and Lily-Rose.

One Saturday when we were coming back from one of our Mexico trips, I thought I would ask Bella about her upbringing. After all, our wait at the border was going to be an estimated two and half hours, so I figured we had the time. And so I asked.

Bella told me she felt her parents were always there for her. She felt she could express her emotions freely and both her mom and dad would listen. When I asked some questions specific to her dad, her eyes lit up. She said, "I remember my dad always being there." And then she took a moment and paused. "I don't ever remember my dad being on his cell phone when I needed to talk with him. Sure, there were times he had to answer an important call, but he would say he would call them back. I felt safe and secure around my dad. And we still have a great relationship to this day."

The relationally secure person, in this case Bella, would answer the questions *Am I worthy of love?* and *Am I capable of others loving me?* with a resounding *yes*!

This type of upbringing creates a positive view of not only themselves, but also others. The fact that Bella's parents were willing to listen to her, made time for her, and allowed her to freely express emotions, created closeness and independence. Bella now feels safe to explore what God has in store for her. She feels secure and confident in opening up and sharing emotions when appropriate. Clinton and Straub summarize secure people as people who

- Are not afraid of emotions, their own or anyone else's
- Are willing to seek and accept comfort from other people
- Know that relationships can be safe, and that knowledge gives them courage to engage in love and intimacy

- Take responsibility for themselves
- Find the courage to act when action is needed[3]

Anxious Attachment

Stefan's parents divorced when he was ten years of age. Often he would comment that his parents would fight over who would get to spend time with him. There were even times when his dad would punish him for wanting to spend time with his mom. At times Stefan felt it was his job to be strong for his parents when they were feeling down. He felt his parents' needs were more important than his.

Looking back, Stefan can see how his parents were emotionally immature and put him in positions he should never have been in. And as a result, he does not have high self-esteem or a lot of drive to pursue his dreams. Those with an anxious relationship style "crave closeness, but they are seldom secure in any relationship, even when others have proven over and over that they really care."[4]

Those with this relational attachment style do not feel worthy of love. Whether it is feeling worthy of love in a romantic relationship or even with God, something inside these people tells them that it is all an illusion, that they really aren't worthy of others' love. In answering the two central questions— *Am I worthy of love?* and *Am I capable of others loving me?*— the relationally anxious person would say they are not worthy of love, but they generally do feel that others care about them. Those whose relationships are shaped by their anxiety:

- Long for intimacy but live in constant, nagging fear of rejection
- Are very needy, desperately looking for others to make them feel safe and secure

- Trust too easily and unwisely, overlooking signs that others have not earned their trust
- Are fragile and vulnerable to any perceived criticism, interpreting it as severe rejection
- Hope that authority figures will finally come through and fix their problems
- Experience a deep, controlling fear that they are not competent to make it on their own[5]

Avoidant Attachment

Raul has an avoidant attachment style. I have known Raul since he was born, and I have seen his parents raise him. His parents were well-meaning and wanted Raul to have a sense of strength and independence; consequently, whenever Raul cried out asking for help or when he fell and scraped his knee, they would say, "Suck it up." When he would try to express how he felt, he would not feel as if he was heard, and he never felt validated. As Raul is now in his early twenties, he believes that he has to do everything on his own because, he feels, no one is there to support or assist him.

"Avoidants tend to develop their emotional energies to competition at work, in sports, and in politics, and they express intense anger over losses and joy in victories."[6] They are always trying to prove their worth by their accomplishments—and the more they achieve, the more they feel love. In Raul's situation, when he excels at his work or in recreational sports, he tends to arrogantly brag. Completely the opposite of those with anxious attachment, avoidants would say they are worthy of love, but that when it comes down to it, others do not really care about them. Those who have an avoidant relational attachment style

- Avoid intimacy because they do not see the need for it
- Are confident in their abilities and are self-reliant
- Commonly experience low levels of anxiety in relationships, even when others are very needy and demanding
- Are very analytical about those in authority, and seldom trust others very much
- Withdraw from those who express emotional needs
- Have, in effect, business relationships with others, even close family members, with clear expectations of what each person will do to make a relationship work[7]

Fearful Attachment

Elaine from Chapter Five comes to mind when I think of fearful attachment. When she came into my office at the beginning of her senior year, Elaine was fearful to share her story. Since I was an authority figure, she was not sure how I would respond to her life story—but at the same time, she came into my office because she wanted to trust again. Additionally, because I am the campus pastor, she felt somewhat safe in sharing. Her home life was marked by being verbally abused by her father and her neighbor sexually violating her. She rarely felt safe at home, and in fact, she faced most days in survival mode.

Those who identify with the fearful attachment relationship style do not believe they are worthy of love or of having others love them. And some do not even have the confidence or drive needed to excel in life. Fearful people have often been hurt and still have open emotional wounds that have not healed; consequently, they have developed a protective shell around their hearts to keep others out. "They long to trust someone, but they have difficulty trusting even those who have proven to be loving and honorable."[8] People who express fearful attachment

- Feel unloved and unwanted, unworthy of anyone's affection
- Long for real relationships, but are terrified of being close
- Lack confidence in their abilities to make life work
- Are fragile, easily shattered, and vulnerable to any perceived offense
- Believe they need to trust those in authority, but simply cannot
- Sometimes remain isolated, but sometimes launch out into relationships, seeking the connection they have always wanted (but their neediness almost always drives people away)[9]

As you look over the four relational attachment styles, do you see yourself in any of them? While some people have more affinity to one style, others are a mixture of these styles. Yet, no matter what style or mixture of styles you might be, remember this—your style is not permanent, nor does it define who you are. No matter what has happened in the past, God can heal and redeem you. You do not have to be a prisoner to the past; you can have a new start! God is not done with us. We are clay in

> **Share This**
>
> No matter what has happened in the past, God can heal and redeem you. You do not have to be a prisoner to the past; you can have a new start!
>
> #everyonelovessex

the hands of the master potter (Isa. 64:8). He molds us, mends us, and heals us. As the clay, however, it is our responsibility to allow God to heal us. We place ourselves in a position to be healed through a number of avenues, including spiritual disciplines, forgiveness, community, and professional counseling.

In my capacity working with college students, I have had the opportunity to talk with thousands of people about what is going on in their lives—about life, relationships, work, and love. I have heard more heart-wrenching stories than I care to recount. But I have also heard stories of God redeeming and restoring. My favorite encounters are those where I see growth in students. Sometimes I will meet with a student regularly or semi-regularly for a year or more. Those whom I have had the privilege of meeting with for multiple years, I try to help them see the progress they have made, pointing out major milestones of growth. For some, it is difficult for them to see where they have grown (partly because of their past and their subsequent relational attachment style); others, however, when they take a step back can see the road they have traveled and the growth and healing along the way. They can clearly see where they were—and where they are today. They can see the tough decisions made and the places of healing in their lives. As you read through the attachment styles, you may have thought there's no hope for you—that you are permanently scarred from the past. I can tell you from firsthand experience that there is always hope.[10]

The Four Loves

We use the word "love" for just about anything. Just the other day I said, "I love Mexican food," and then later that night I told my wife and daughters that I love them. Love is powerful—books are written about it, people sing about it—but the meaning of love can be diluted. And that is partly why we confuse love and sex. So what is love?

The New Testament was written in Greek, the language Alexander the Great spread after he conquered much of the known world. What is fascinating about Greek is that depending on the word and context, words can have a truly robust meaning. For example, in the English language we have one word for love—that's it! That one word sums up our love for our spouse and Mexican food. However, in Greek there are actually four different words for love. So it is pretty important that we know these four words in order to know what kind of love we are talking about.

> **The Four Loves**
> **Storge:** Affection Love
> **Phileo:** Friendship Love
> **Eros:** Romantic Love
> **Agape:** Divine Love

The first type of love is referred to in Greek as *storge*. This kind of love is closest to the idea we speak of in saying, "I love being with my family." This kind of love appears when there is deep familiarity. My three-year-old daughter "loves" our cat, Vegemite (Yes, we really named him that! The two other cats we had were named Crikey and Roo), not because he is the most loving and selfless cat, but because he is familiar to her. She has known Vegemite (the cat, not the food) since she was born. *Storge* is a safe, comfortable, good-feeling type of love. It is the "I like being around you" type of love.[11]

A second kind of love—friendship love—is represented in the Greek word *phileo*. This type of love is based either on common interests or common sufferings—something that connects two people. This love does not really have anything to do with social standing, but rather points to a common goal. "Friendship is unnecessary, like philosophy, like art, like the universe itself (for God did not need to create it). It has no survival value; rather it is one of those things which give value to survival."[12]

The love that we have been talking about in this book is a third kind—*eros*—that we talk about when we say that we "are in love." "Plato will have it that 'falling in love' is the mutual recognition on earth of souls which have been singled out for one another in a precious and celestial existence."[13] In other words, this is the kind of love that is often spoken of as finding your soul mate.

The idea of finding a "soul mate" originates in Greek mythology. Plato wrote that each human being originally had four arms, one head, but two faces, and four legs. The way the legend goes is that humanity was getting too strong and growing in number, so the gods in the pantheon, led by Zeus, decided to have us cut in half. So now we are in a desperate search the world over for our other half—our perfect match.[14] Obviously this is merely a legend, but so is the idea of there being only one "the one." The one is the one you choose to marry and work together with through the good times and the bad times. This is what love is all about. A singular soul mate is simply a product of Greek mythology.

> **Share This**
> The idea of finding a "soul mate" originates in Greek mythology.
> #everyonelovessex

There is a final word for love in Greek: *agape*. This is the word that is often used for God's faithful and unending love. It is also often translated as charity or even referred to as divine love. When you read 1 Corinthians 13, what is often referred to as the love chapter, you are reading about the *agape* type of love. This love gives us the ability to love the unlovable— and expect nothing back. This type of love, however, scares people so much that some would rather run or hide from love. Sadly, when we run from this kind of love, we lose a part of ourselves—a part of who we were created to be. C. S. Lewis puts it this way:

> To love at all is to be vulnerable. Love anything, and your heart will certainly be wrung and possibly be broken. If you want to make sure of keeping it intact, you must give your heart to no one, not even to an animal. . . . lock it up safe in the casket or coffin of your selfishness. But in that casket—safe, dark, motionless, airless—it will change. It will not be broken; it will become unbreakable, impenetrable, irredeemable. . . . The only place outside Heaven where you can be perfectly safe from all the dangers and perturbations of love is Hell.[15]

Let's put this *agape* kind of love in the perspective of the entire Bible. It starts from the very beginning with Adam and Eve. When God created humanity, he gave us free will, meaning the ability and absolute freedom to either obey or disobey God. Sometimes people question why God would give us free will; after all, free will causes murders, hate crimes, abuse, and a whole host of other things. Put into the context of *agape* love, the gift of free will is an act of true love, because without free will, we would be reduced to robots, programmed to follow God out of duty. God wants our love out of free will, out of our *choice* to follow and love him.

When Caz and I started dating, we fell in love over time—and we chose to commit to each other for the rest of our lives. There was no coercion or force involved. Imagine if when we started dating I had gone to her and said in a forceful voice, "You will love me! Or else!" Am I offering her true love? Would her response be one of true love or of fear? True love can never be based on fear or coercion. True love is always rooted in choice. Without choice, without freedom and free will, true love would never exist. The point is that in order for there to be true love, there must be a choice.

From the beginning of creation, God has been reaching out to humanity. He has been wooing humanity unto himself, inviting humanity into a relationship of love and loyalty to him. From the singular person of Abraham to the tribe of Jacob to the entire Hebrew people, God has been on a mission of reaching out to humanity. But the story did not end in the Hebrew Bible; it carried on into the New Testament, where we see another of God's great acts of love—Jesus. It is because of Jesus' death, burial, and resurrection that we have been freed from sin and death. Moreover, in Jesus, God offers us the chance to be made whole again—to be redeemed, delivered, healed—to experience *shalom*, peace and wholeness. All of this has been his desire from the very beginning.

So What Does All This Have to Do with Sex?

How we view love has a central role to play in what we think about sex. If we merely view love through the lens of *eros*, sex can be reduced to a self-gratifying act. However, if we see love as a part of *agape*—a love that is connected, intimate, and giving—then sex becomes something wholly different. In other words, if sex was unwanted and coerced, this will have implications for what sex means to you. But if sex is set within the larger scope of agape love, sex becomes the beautiful gift God intended it to be.

Sex is God's gift us to us! It's a gift that unites and bonds—and one of the most powerful forces on earth. When sex is connected in marriage—as God designed it—there's an emotional, spiritual, and physical bonding that's unlike anything else. When God created Adam and Eve, they did not have shame from their nakedness. In other words, Adam and Eve were psychologically, spiritually, and emotionally open without any shame. They lived in a harmonious relationship with God and each other.[16]

Although sex is a gift, sadly for many people their first experience with sex was anything but "a gift." In our world today, sex is a recreational activity, done at random with pretty much whomever we want. True love does not work that way. Sex can draw people together, whether for a night or a season. Love, however, is quite the opposite. Love draws us together in a way that is deeper than recreational sex. When that person is not there, we are sad, lonely, and heartbroken. Sex accounts for having babies. Love accounts for the ability to build community.[17]

Some people use sex as an instrument to find love. I read a story where

> **Share This**
>
> If sex was unwanted and coerced, this will have implications for what sex means to you. But if sex is set within the larger scope of *agape* love, sex becomes the beautiful gift God intended it to be.
>
> #everyonelovessex

one college-age girl slept with men to find love, and after twenty or so partners, she was not any closer to finding love than when she started. Searching for meaning or love through sex is like searching for a needle in a haystack. It simply does not happen. Sex, it is sometimes believed, will lead us to love. That is like one saying if he or she would just sleep with me, then I will be complete or then I know they will fall in love with me. It just does not happen that way. Rabbi Shmuley Boteach summarizes this well: "It appears as those who have sex today rarely have the capacity to change the way a man and a woman feel about each other. It is pleasurable and enjoyable while it lasts, but quickly dissipates thereafter."[18]

> **Share This**
> Searching for meaning or love through sex is like searching for a needle in a haystack.
> #everyonelovessex

The only thing that guarantees two people will live together, grow together, and learn together is love, not sex. As Rabbi Boteach reminds us, "It is love that makes marriage and not sex."[19] Sex in the midst of marriage is what God designed. Sex in the midst of love is what the couple in Song of Songs was rejoicing over. Sex in the midst of love is what ultimately makes sex fulfilling, holy, and sacred. This type of fulfilling sex only comes through marriage—a marriage where your beloved finding you is so special and unique that they would rather spend the vast majority of their remaining time on earth with you than with any other person.[20]

Scratches and Make-Believe

When I officiate weddings, one of the most powerful moments is when couples express to one another their promises to love, honor, and be intimate with only that person—for the rest of their lives. It is pretty much the biggest commitment anyone can ever make. Through their vows they are promising that every aspect of their love will only be to the other. These vows are solidified or sealed with rings. Below is what I generally say in referring to the power of the wedding rings:

> As I look at these rings I wish I could pray a blessing over them that would ensure a blissful and conflict-free marriage for the rest of your lives. Instead of arguing, you two would do nothing but praise each other. Instead of slamming the door and storming off to the other room, you would always hold and comfort each other. I wish that I could pray this blessing and the two of you would live happily ever after—but it would not be reality. The reality is that marriage has its ups and downs, arguments and joys What these rings are is a symbol of the commitment you two are making today. I wish I could pray some magical blessing on them—but that would be make-believe.
>
> As your marriage moves through the years, I want you both to constantly look at your rings and remember the commitment and love you two have for one another right now. As I look at the rings I notice that they are beautiful, shiny, and flawless. However, in a few years you will notice that your rings are not as shiny or impeccable as they once were. In fact, you will notice dings and scratches on them—and that's okay. Those dings and scratches tell the story of your marriage. They tell about your ups and downs—and that through it all, the two of

you worked on building a stronger relationship and a healthier marriage. Even though you had your ups and downs, your lows and highs, you stuck it out. You held one another with such high respect that you did not leave, but rather worked it out. Your relationship was tested, but you were able to get through it—together—and these rings will tell the story of your commitment.

So, cherish these rings, cherish the marriage bed, and cherish one another. And when you do that, you will have a fulfilling life—emotionally, spiritually, and sexually! A life where others will look at you and say, "They have something powerful!"

This is what marriage *can* be—and sex is a big part of it. Sex within marriage is not a second-rate experience. In fact, it is the highest expression of love, true agape love. It can be the very best sex of your life—filled with love, intimacy, and connection—a giving and beautiful experience unlike any other. This is what sex was meant to be—the gift that God intended. As Rabbi Boteach so beautifully observes, "Intimate sex done right elevates what can be an indulgent, animalistic human practice to a higher plane, where we realize the full glory of being human."[21]

> **Share This**
> Sex within marriage is not a second-rate experience. In fact, it is the highest expression of love, true *agape* love.
> #everyonelovessex

CONTINUING THE DISCUSSION

1. Why are love and sex so powerful?

2. Are sex and love the same thing?

3. How do you define *love*?

4. There are four relational or attachment styles: Secure Attachment, Anxious Attachment, Avoidant Attachment, and Fearful Attachment. Which one are you?

5. Do you believe true love always requires a choice? Why or why not?

6. Do you believe there is "the one" out there for you?

Have you shared your thoughts online yet?
#EveryoneLovesSex

Notes

[1] C. B. Thomas and K. R. Duszynski, "Closeness to Parents and the Family Constellation in a Prospective Study of Five Disease States: Suicide, Mental Illness, Malignant Tumors, Hypertension, and Coronary Heart Disease," *Johns Hopkins Medical Journal* 134.5 (1974): 251–70.

[2] Tim Clinton and Joshua Straub, *God Attachment: Why You Believe, Act, and Feel the Way You Do About God* (New York: Howard Books, 2010), 66–67.

[3] Ibid., 70.

[4] Ibid., 71.

[5] Ibid., 70–71.

[6] Ibid., 72.

[7] Ibid., 73.

[8] Ibid., 74.

[9] Ibid.

[10] Two books that have literally changed my life and brought me emotional healing are *Boundaries: When to Say Yes, How to Say No to Take Control of Your Life* (Grand Rapids: Zondervan, 1992) by Dr. Henry Cloud and Dr. John Townsend, and *The DNA of Relationships* (Carol Stream, IL: Tyndale, 2007) by Dr. Gary Smalley. I offer these resources to you because they had such a positive impact on my life.

[11] C. S. Lewis, *The Four Loves* (New York: Harcourt Brace, 1960), 31–33.

[12] Ibid., 71.

[13] Ibid., 108.

[14] Plato, *Symposium*, trans. Benjamin Jowett, e-book, http://classics.mit.edu/Plato/symposium.html.

[15] Lewis, *The Four Loves*, 121.

[16] Tremper Longman III, "A Return to Eden: Redeeming Sexuality," *Westmont Magazine*, Spring 2011, http://blogs.westmont.edu/magazine/2011/07/21/a-return-to-eden-redeeming-sexuality/.

[17] Shmuley Boteach, *Kosher Sex: A Recipe for Passion and Intimacy* (New York: Broadway Books, 2001), 22.

[18] Ibid., 34.

[19] Ibid., 22.

[20] Ibid., 4.

[21] Ibid., 29.

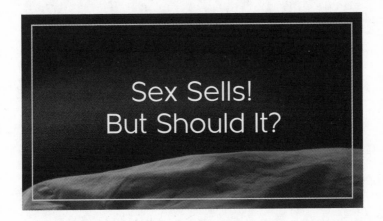

CHAPTER 7

Sex Sells!
But Should It?

Even in Detroit

Theresa's story begins when she was a fifteen-year-old, blonde-haired, blue-eyed girl living in an upper-middle-class suburb of Detroit. There was not a lot of crime in her neighborhood, making it a safe haven to grow up in, or so she thought. She had a mom and a dad, family, and friends. Everything seemed normal—until predators targeted her.

When Theresa was in high school, she was targeted by a group of guys, some of whom she attended high school with. They would pay her compliments and show her positive affection, all in an effort to build her trust in them. After six months of this behavior, one of the guys asked Theresa if she wanted a ride home. "I jumped at the chance, because by then I had a crush on him, and I thought everything would be fine. But he didn't take me home." Instead he took Theresa to his house and invited her in. "No, no, no. I'm good," Theresa told him nervously. But he insisted, "But come on, I like you." The young man tried to smooth things over to make Theresa comfortable, so he offered her a soda. Little did she know that the soda was laced with some sort of drug. Within a short period of time she was incapacitated from the drug—and he raped her. Pictures were taken of the sex act.

Jeira's Story–"I Hate My Life Now!"

"The people that trafficked me told me that I was going to London for a holiday. I was excited, because I had never traveled outside [the country], but my excitement was quickly replaced by dread when I landed in the city. I was forced to have sex with men and threatened with beatings if I refused. I eventually escaped. I hate my life now, and I regularly use drink and drugs."[1]

He brought her back home and threatened that if she told anyone, her family would be killed. I can only imagine the terror and fright of this helpless teenage girl. Not only was she sexually violated, but pictures were taken, and now she was responsible for her family's survival. She kept all this a secret—from her family, from everyone. For the next two years, under threat of harm to her family, Theresa was their sex slave. They allowed her to live at home, but would take her out at night to have her sleep with other men. Her traffickers were profiting off the pictures they were taking of her as well as the prostitution she was forced into.

Theresa would be taken to very elite homes as well as run-down motels around midnight, where she would wait for men to come in to rape her. This would happen for hours—and then around three in the morning they would take her home. She would get a few hours of sleep, wake up around six or seven, and then go to school. Remember, some of these guys went to her high school!

One night, after two years of this constant trafficking abuse, the group took Theresa to an inner-city Detroit motel, where they had about twenty guys waiting to rape her. She was sixteen or seventeen around this time. "I think they had full intention of coming back to get me—but never returning me home ever again." After everyone had left, and before the traffickers came back, she fled the dingy motel and just started walking. Luckily, a server at a small diner saw her and asked if she needed help. The police were called. Theresa was free, and she and her family have moved away from the upper-middle-class area they once considered safe.

Theresa started an organization called S.O.A.P., which stands for Save Our Adolescents from Prostitution. "I realized on my worst nights when I had been taken to that motel and left for dead that I really could have used someone to talk to. And these girls don't know they are human trafficking victims. They don't know there is a hotline number out there. And so I decided that I was going to get them this phone number so they can talk to somebody in their worst moments, which is generally in the motels where they are being sold over and over again."[2] Theresa puts a hotline phone number on soap bars in motels and hotels, and also talks with the managers about the reality of human trafficking. Women have seen the bars of soap with the phone number wrapped around the bar and have called, asking for help.

After two years of physical, emotional, and sexual abuse, Theresa escaped. She has been through counseling, is still healing, but now speaks out against the horrific monstrosity and has written a book about her experience, *The Slave Across the Street*. Theresa, a daughter in a well-off family in a well-off neighborhood, experienced more pain in two years than anyone should ever have to experience in a lifetime. She experienced the reality that sex sells. Her traffickers made money off the media they were selling of her as well as the multiple men who would pay to rape her.

What Human Trafficking Looks Like

Human trafficking is one of the world's fastest-growing global crimes, with 5.5 million children being trafficked worldwide every year.[3] This is not only an issue in underdeveloped countries, but is actually a growing issue right here in our backyard—literally happening in our neighborhoods, even in *nice* neighborhoods like Theresa's. The U.S. Department of Health and Human Services states:

> The data and methodologies for estimating the prevalence of human trafficking globally and nationally are not well developed, and therefore estimates have varied widely and changed significantly over time. The U.S. State Department has estimated that approximately 600,000 to 800,000 victims are trafficked annually across international borders worldwide and approximately half of these victims are younger than age 18 (U.S. Department of State, 2005, 2006, 2007). Additionally, the U.S. State Department has estimated that 80 percent of internationally trafficked victims are female and 70 percent are trafficked into the sex industry.[4]

The United Nations Office on Drugs and Crime defines human trafficking as "the recruitment, transport, transfer, harboring or receipt of a person by such means as threat or use of force or other forms of coercion, of abduction, of fraud or deception for the purpose of exploitation."[5] In the case of Theresa, she was "recruited," locally transported, and was coerced into heinous sex crimes against her. Because of her traffickers' exploitation of her, they profited. It should also be stated briefly that sex trafficking is not the only form of human trafficking.

There are two main forms of human trafficking: forced labor and sex trafficking. Labor traffickers use threats, lies, and bondage—any form of coercion to force people to work against their will. We see forced laborers in the United States and abroad working to make clothes, chocolate, or anything else that will make the traffickers a profit. Labor trafficking, like sex trafficking, devalues people, treating them as less than human.

The most common form of human trafficking is sex exploitation. The United Nations has reported, however, that this may be a statistical bias, because it is possible that sex trafficking is more reported than labor trafficking. Some of the other forms of human trafficking that are underreported are forced or bonded labor, domestic servitude, forced marriage, organ removal, and the exploitation of children in begging.[6]

While there is no one way in which sex trafficking happens, the sad reality is that it does happen. The good news is that we have seen in the last ten years

— Share This —

And for the first time in world history, religious leaders from around the world signed a commitment against human trafficking. Their goal is to eradicate human trafficking by the year 2020.

#everyonelovessex

or so a real movement of churches and nonprofit organizations getting behind this cause. These groups are trying to stop the exploitation of people, putting a stop to selling women, children, and men for their profit. In 2007, the Senate slated January 11 as "National Human Trafficking Awareness Day."[7] In 2015, President Obama issued a presidential proclamation declaring January 2016 "National Slavery and Human Trafficking Prevention Month."[8] And for the first time in world history, religious leaders from around the world signed a commitment against human trafficking. Their goal is to eradicate human trafficking by the year 2020.[9] Yet with all this involvement and awareness, the sad reality is that the demand to exploit human beings *continues* to rise.

All I Wanted Was to Be Loved!

"Wendy Barnes was 15 years old the first time she met Greg, a sixteen-year-old high school junior who would ultimately become the father of her three children and force her to accept a life in prostitution [sex slavery] for 12 years. 'All I wanted was to be loved,' writes Wendy in a personal email. 'I wanted to be special to someone.'"[10]

Pornography and Sex Trafficking

I think it is quite accurate to say that human trafficking is a global, religious, political, and human rights issue. What many do not know, however, is that there is a connection between pornography and human trafficking in creating the demand.

As one watches pornography, the reward center of the brain is activated, and the more porn watched, the less that part of the brain is activated. Consequently, one must watch something more extreme in order to get that original sensation.[11]

The more pornography one watches, the more likely they are to get addicted and will need more to watch. And considering that twelve is the average age a child starts viewing pornography, that's a lot of pornographic images.

There is a natural progression to pornography. One thing leads to another: soft-core pornography leads to hard-core pornography; fetish pornography leads to bondage and abusive pornography, and so on. Your brain releases chemicals that "reward" the brain, causing the need to watch more and stronger pornography to get the same reward. The result is that the "reward" is working against you—just like a drug. In fact, the part of the brain that is activated when pornography is being watched is the same part of the brain that is activated under the influence of drugs.[12]

Pornography creates an environment where the explicit abuse and disrespect of women is acceptable. Part of the challenge in fighting against the pornography industry is combating the popularity or normality of pornography use among so many. In fact, can you think of any of your friends who you know absolutely for sure do not watch pornography? Sadly, it is difficult for many of us to think of even one friend. Additionally, we must fight against the well-received belief that pornography is perfectly acceptable to watch as long as it is *consenting adults* watching—and that pornography will sexually satisfy the one watching it.[13]

> **Share This**
> There are two links between pornography consumption and human trafficking.
> #everyonelovessex

There are two links between pornography consumption and human trafficking. First, thousands of children and women are forced into pornography, whether it appears consensual or not. Second, those who watch pornography eventually become desensitized to what's on the screen, which results in a searching for sexual encounters outside of the home to fulfill the "reward" cycle.[14] In this way, pornography becomes a gateway act—one that can take someone where they never thought they would end up—to the possibility of hiring a sex trafficking victim.[15]

━Share This━

"We know that trafficking is increasing—which means demand is increasing. This means that men are increasingly willing to have sex with women who are being controlled and abused by pimps and traffickers."

#everyonelovessex

In 2016, the Tennessee Bureau of Investigation made headlines across the nation as its agents apprehended thirty-two men and women in a three-day human trafficking and prostitution sting. They posted ads on www .backpage.com, where agents posed as underage girls ready to have sex. The chief of police said the sting was "designed to identify and help victims of trafficking, as well as take these predators off the street." Thirty-two men and women answered the ad and actually showed up to have sex with the underage child and were arrested. Those arrested included a volunteer firefighter, an engineer, and two pastors.[16] Regarding the arrests, the police chief commented, "Human trafficking is a scourge on society. We will continue to commit all the necessary resources and work alongside our law enforcement partners to help protect our most precious resource, our children."[17]

It would be sobering to interview these prospective child molesters and ask them about their involvement in pornography, as the odds are that they all watched pornography of some type. In a *Huffington Post* interview, professor of sociology and women's studies at Wheelock College, and self-proclaimed "radical feminist," Dr. Gail Dines, states, "We know that trafficking is increasing—which means demand is increasing. This means that men are increasingly willing to have sex with women who are being controlled and abused by pimps and traffickers."[18] Professor Dines says that leads us to one of two conclusions. One conclusion is that it is just in man's biology to do this to women. The second conclusion is that "they are being socialized by the culture to lose all empathy for women." In regard to Dines's first conclusion she says, "I refuse to accept that men are born rapists, porn users, or johns."[19]

Here's what happened to sex trafficking survivor Anna Malika.

Situations Vary for Everyone Trafficked

"The situations that sex trafficking victims face vary dramatically. Many victims become romantically involved with someone who then forces or manipulates them into prostitution. Others are lured in with false promises of a job, such as modeling or dancing. Some are forced to sell sex by their parents or other family members. They may be involved in a trafficking situation for a few days or weeks, or may remain in the same trafficking situation for years."[20]

"The Art Project"

Anna was born in Calcutta, India, and was adopted into an American family. At eight years of age, her adoptive parents divorced. Her mom remarried, and that new husband beat her mom and was abusive in many ways toward her. Her dad, after the divorce, had lots of different relationships. Women were always coming and going with her dad. All that to say, she did not have a lot of stability. Nor did she receive a lot of love, acceptance, or validation from her parents.

> Being Indian, I never really felt like I belonged any-
> where. I did not have a sense of belonging. I always
> wanted to be white, because I thought if I was white,
> I would be beautiful and worthy of good things. So
> I had this instability over here, and I also had this
> desire to be wanted and needed.

In high school, she never felt like she belonged. She compared herself, her clothes, her skin color, to every girl she encoun-tered. Because she wasn't white, felt like she was not skinny enough, and did not get attention from parents, she felt alone and isolated. In her junior year of high school, Anna got a job at a movie theater. One of the projection operators offered her free guitar lessons, and she jumped with enthusiasm at the opportunity. Over time, this co-worker, who was forty years of age, started complimenting Anna, saying she was beautiful and talented—words she desperately longed to hear. "All these things [words of affirmation] I've been desperately wanting to hear for so very long. These lessons became more roman-tic. It never crossed my mind that he was in his forties and I was a teenager. All that mattered was that I wanted to spend more time with him."

They started spending time together, a lot of time together. So much time that she noticed she wasn't spending any more time with any of her other friends, and he was pressuring her to always be with him. During this time, Anna was kicked out of her house because of her behavior and had nowhere to go. The forty-year-old co-worker—and now boyfriend—offered that she could move in with him. It made sense to her. Anna thought, "We're dating and in love. And I'm important to him!" So they moved in together.

One day he asked her to be part of his "art project." He told her that she could be his number-one model! With a smile and a sense of validation in her tone, she agreed. "I began this art project that was very innocent at first, and then it became more sexual as time went on. I was forced to do unthinkable things. I was forced to do things that were very violent."

Things continued to get stranger. On his refrigerator, he had a calendar that detailed all of their sex acts, so she asked him about it. "It's just how many times we made love," he replied. Anna reasoned that this was acceptable, reminding herself that he would never lie to her. Other times Anna would wake up naked and not know where she had been. Somehow she knew she had been sexually violated. Again, she asked him about it. "You were just sleepwalking," he said.

As this continued, he became more possessive—not wanting her to leave his sight and even controlling her money. She recalled a time when they went shopping and she went one aisle over in the grocery store, and he freaked out. He told her, "Where did you go! Don't leave me. I love you and want to be with you all the time!" At this time in her life, all that mattered was that someone showed her love and attention—vital emotions she had never received. "All that mattered is that he wanted me. For once in my life I was wanted and I was told I was beautiful. And I belonged somewhere! That's all that mattered to me!"

As time went on, he started talking about marriage, which scared Anna. One of Anna's co-workers needed a roommate, and Anna decided to move in with her. When her boyfriend was gone one day, she gathered all her belongings and left him.

She never saw him again. He tried to find out where she was, but she went off the grid. Sadly, her story does not end there.

One day she received a call that her former boyfriend had

Recognize the Signs of Human Trafficking

The following are just some of the warning signs of human trafficking:

- Is not free to leave or come and go as he/she wishes
- Is under 18 and is providing commercial sex acts
- Is in the commercial sex industry and has a pimp/ manager
- Is unpaid, paid very little, or paid only through tips
- Works excessively long and/or unusual hours
- Is not allowed breaks or suffers under unusual restrictions at work
- Owes a large debt and is unable to pay it off
- Was recruited through false promises concerning the nature and conditions of his/her work
- High-security measures exist in the work and/or living locations (e.g., opaque windows, boarded-up windows, bars on windows, barbed wire, security cameras, etc.)[21]

---

died of cancer. She wanted to get the pictures back from his "art project," and the only way she knew how to do that was to go to the funeral and ask. One of his family members took her to the house and handed her a big box. When she got home, she opened the box—and discovered that he had mass-produced every picture.

Anna's boyfriend was selling the images of the two of them having sex. People looking at the images would not know whether it was consensual or it was forced. Her trafficker had a huge addiction to pornography. His bedroom was filled with pornography, every type imaginable. Anna explains, "His addiction desensitized his mind to the point where he would say, 'Let's do what these girls did in this video.' His porn addiction was fueling his drive to exploit me."[22]

Anna went on a downward spiral, started drinking, and started cutting. Depressed and angry, she hated herself. Realizing that she was heading down the wrong course, she reached out to Mercy Ministries, who helped her in her healing process. Today, she is study-

> **━Share This━**
> Human trafficking victims are not just people we see on the streets; it can happen to anyone.
> #everyonelovessex

ing sociology and pre-law, and continues to reach out to those trapped in sex trafficking. Her message is simple: human trafficking victims are not just people we see on the streets; it can happen to anyone. Anna was still going to school—and being trafficked. Moreover, she didn't even realize she was being trafficked—and sadly, this is more common than we would like to admit.

I wonder how many other porn clips on the Internet are from trafficked victims. In one study, nearly half of those trafficked said pornography was made of them while they were in prostitution. And this survey was taken in nine different countries.[23] Fight the New Drug, an organization made up of advocates and experts committed to stopping human trafficking, writes this about porn and trafficking:

> The pornography industry works hard to keep up a glamorous image, but behind the camera is a reality of violence, drugs, and human trafficking. With

some editing and off-screen coercion, pornographers can make it look like what's happening onscreen is being enjoyed. But the uncut version is a different story. Remember, clicking it is supporting it. Refuse to click, and stop the demand for porn and sex trafficking.[24]

Shameful Statistics

- 63 percent of underage sex trafficking victims said they had been advertised or sold online.
- The average age of entry into the sex trade in America is fourteen to sixteen years old.
- A pimp can make $150,000–$200,000 per child each year and exploits an average of four to six girls.
- One in six endangered runaways reported to the National Center for Missing and Exploited Children in 2013 were likely sex trafficking victims.[25]

What If?

It can be frustrating to hear about a problem and not have any solutions or possibilities. Working in the church world for thirteen years and in the university world since 2011, I have heard my share of issues and causes the church needs to address. Over the years I have started to respond by asking a simple question: "What can I do about it?"

Regardless of your age, your past, your insecurities, or whatever is holding you back, you can make a difference. If you feel too young, remember the words the apostle Paul wrote to Timothy, "Don't let anyone look down on you because you are young, but set an example for the believers in speech, in conduct, in love, in faith and in purity" (1 Tim. 4:12). God has a habit of using those who are young and willing to do big things. Just ask Mary.

Maybe you feel like you have nothing to offer. If so, remember the biblical account where Jesus contrasted the widow who gave two copper pennies with the rich. Jesus said, "This poor widow has put in more than all the others. All these people gave their gifts out of their wealth; but she out of her poverty put in all she had to live on" (Luke 21:3–4). God has a different way of measuring what we think we may or may not have. He simply wants us to be willing to give what we have.

> **Share This**
> Regardless of your age, your past, your insecurities, or whatever is holding you back, you can make a difference.
> #everyonelovessex

Maybe you feel inadequate. If so, remember the stories of Esther or Moses. Esther felt inadequate to talk to the king about the destruction of her people. Moses felt inadequate about going to pharaoh, the king of Egypt. In both stories we find God using people in spite of their perceived inadequacies. Apparently God has a different outlook on what we can and cannot do.

You have gifts and abilities. You have friends and connections. You have passion and drive. You have love and compassion. You have technology and the ability to use it. You have a voice. And most importantly, you have a willingness to use what you have to put an end to sex trafficking. We all could make a difference—by living a life that brings justice and a voice to those who have been unjustly treated and have no voice. We can live a life of action, doing our part in stopping what breaks God's heart. Here are four steps you can take right now to make a difference:

Step #1–Stop Supporting the Porn Industry

As we have seen, pornography adds to the demand. Pornography desensitizes us to the horrors of sex slaves and the abuse of women. Pornography dehumanizes people, making them mere objects of passion and conquest. Two great websites helping those with an addiction to pornography are www.xxxchurch .com and www.restoringthesoul.com.

Step #2–Get Involved with Human Trafficking Organizations

There are many great organizations combating human trafficking. You can get involved with an organization called Stop the Traffic (http://www.stopthetraffik.org/usa). Another organization that focuses on policy changes, supporting stronger state and federal laws, is the Polaris Project (www.polarisproject .org). The Polaris Project also operates the National Human Trafficking Resource Center hotline (888-373-7888) and the Be Free text line (text "BeFree" to 233733).

Step #3–Create an Awareness Group

Begin to meet weekly, maybe as a small group that is connected with your church, to discuss the horrors of human trafficking and what you can do as a group to put an end to it. You can find a small-group curriculum at https://www.ijm.org/resources.

Step #4–Pray

Often our first response can be to charge into a situation full-steam ahead! I would highly suggest that you gather with others who have the same concern and pray. Pray for direction in what you should do as a group to end the horrific crime of human trafficking. Pray for (and act upon) ways to create awareness in your community. Pray for tangible opportunities to make a difference in the lives of real people who are trapped in human trafficking—here and abroad. Together, we really can make a difference.

CONTINUING THE DISCUSSION

1. What were one or two new concepts you learned about human trafficking?

2. What is human trafficking? Do you think it could happen in your neighborhood?

3. What is the connection between pornography and sex trafficking?

4. What are some of the signs in recognizing human trafficking?

5. How can you get involved to stop human trafficking?

6. Why do people enslave others like this?

7. What would Jesus say to the person being trafficked, and what would he say to the trafficker?

Have you shared your thoughts online yet?
#EveryoneLovesSex

Notes

[1]"Stories of Trafficked People: Jeira's Story," Anti-Slavery, http://www
.antislavery.org/english/slavery_today/trafficking/personal_stories_hais
_story.aspx.

[2]"Human Trafficking: A Survivor's Story," Natasha Curry interviews
Theresa Flores on HLN, May 12, 2013, https://www.youtube.com/watch?v
=Oogp8fiJXBU.

[3]"Infographic: A Global Look at Human Trafficking," UNICEF, 2013,
https://www.unicefusa.org/stories/infographic-global-human-trafficking
-statistics.

[4]Heather J. Clawson, Nicole Dutch, Amy Solomon, and Lisa Goldblatt
Grace, "Human Trafficking Into and Within the United States: A Review
of the Literature," U.S. Department of Health and Human Services,
August 30, 2009, https://aspe.hhs.gov/basic-report/human-trafficking
-and-within-united-states-review-literature.

[5]"Human Trafficking FAQ: What Is Human Trafficking?" United
Nations Office on Drugs and Crime, accessed May 31, 2016, http://www
.unodc.org/unodc/en/human-trafficking/faqs.html#What_is_human
_trafficking.

[6]"Human Trafficking FAQ: What Is the Most Common Identified Form
of Trafficking?" United Nations Office on Drugs and Crime, accessed May
31, 2016, http://www.unodc.org/unodc/en/human-trafficking/faqs.html
#What_is_the_most_commonly_identified_form_of_trafficking.

[7]"National Human Trafficking Awareness Day," National Day Calendar,
accessed on May 31, 2016, http://www.nationaldaycalendar.com/
national-human-trafficking-awareness-day-january-11/.

[8]"Presidential Proclamation—National Slavery and Human Trafficking
Prevention Month," The White House, December 31, 2015, https://www
.whitehouse.gov/the-press-office/2015/12/31/presidential-proclamation
-national-slavery-and-human-trafficking.

[9]Guilia Belardelli, "Pope Francis and Other Religious Leaders Sign
Declaration Against Modern Slavery," *Huffington Post*, December 3, 2014,
http://www.huffingtonpost.com/2014/12/02/pope-francis-and-other
-re_n_6256640.html.

[10] Holly Austin Smith, "Sex Trafficking: Should All Perpetrators Be Sentenced as Sex Offenders?" April 21, 2015, http://hollyaustinsmith.com /sex-trafficking-should-all-perpetrators-be-sentenced-as-sex-offenders/.

[11] Cusick, *Surfing for God*, 125–30.

[12] "How Porn Changes the Brain," Fight the New Drug, August 8, 2014, http://www.fightthenewdrug.org/porn-changes-the-brain/.

[13] "Human Trafficking and Pornography," U.S. Catholic Sisters Against Human Trafficking, accessed on May 25, 2016, http://www.stopenslavement .org/studymodules/USCSAHT-03.pdf.

[14] Ibid.

[15] Gottman and Silver, *What Makes Love Last?*, 63–64.

[16] Peter Holley, "Child Sex Sting Nets Two Tennessee Pastors," *Washington Post*, May 24, 2016, http://www.chicagotribune.com/news /nationworld/ct-tennessee-child-sex-sting-pastors-20160524-story.html.

[17] Ibid.

[18] John-Henry Westen, "Want to Stop Sex Trafficking? Look to America's Porn Addiction," *Huffington Post*, last modified March 30, 2015, http:// www.huffingtonpost.com/johnhenry-westen/want-to-stop-sex-traffick _b_6563338.html.

[19] Ibid.

[20] "Sex Trafficking," Polaris Project, accessed on May 31, 2016, https:// polarisproject.org/sex-trafficking.

[21] "Recognize the Signs," Polaris Project, accessed on May 31, 2016, http://polarisproject.org/recognize-signs.

[22] "What's Porn Got to Do with Sex Trafficking? A Survivor Explains," Dawn Hawkins interviews Anna Malika for *Morality in Media*, October 26, 2014, https://www.youtube.com/watch?v=FnPp0DPnb9o.

[23] "How Porn Fuels Sex Trafficking (Video)," Fight the New Drug, March 2, 2015, http://fightthenewdrug.org/how-porn-fuels-sex-trafficking-video/.

[24] Ibid.

[25] "Child Sex Trafficking Statistics," Thorn, accessed on May 31, 2016, https://www.wearethorn.org/child-trafficking-statistics/.

CONCLUSION

Loving Sex More than Ever!

Sexual faithfulness is God's design! It brings fulfillment, builds trust, and strengthens relationships. Sex is not something to think of as dirty but something to celebrate, a gift. At issue is when this gift is misused. When this happens, what was once a beautiful expression translates into untold emotional and psychological damage. So instead of loving sex more than ever, one puts walls up to protect from hurt and harm.

Everyone has a past. Everyone has had struggles. And, for the most part, everyone is good at hiding their past and struggles. You may be surprised at how many of your peers share their past and struggles with me and think they are the only people who struggle. In fact, they would be surprised by how many of their classmates, roommates, and even other adults have the same struggles in their past and current situation—things like unfaithfulness, sexually transmitted diseases, loneliness, insecurities, feeling like failures, depression, anxiety, and trust issues (just to name a few). The reality is that you are not alone—no matter where you are or what you've done or have been through.

> **Share This**
> God is bigger than your struggles—and because of that, there is and will always be hope.
> #everyonelovessex

God is bigger than your struggles—and because of that, there is and will always be hope. As I still have the opportunity to interact with some of the students you read about, I can tell you firsthand—hope and redemption are real. You can find hope, healing, and freedom. Your past does not have to define you—there is a bright future ahead!

When people interact with people you've read about now, they may assume they have it all together and that they have not had any hardships. But that is what happens when we allow God to fully redeem us. He wipes away the tears, heals the wounds, and gives a new sense of purpose and vision for the future. In other words, we are a new creation. But remember, healing from our past does not happen overnight. Be patient!

Politics and Sexual Faithfulness

Politicians have long been criticized for stating that they can accomplish more than they really can. Some call it empty promises, and others call it a reality check when you get into office. Whatever the case, with any candidate who makes it to office, there are always things they will never be able to deliver on.

In the same manner, authors, speakers, and pastors can often "overpromise." We often promise more than what can be delivered—especially in the area of sexual faithfulness. I wish I could assure every reader that if you commit to sexual faithfulness from here on out, you will have the greatest sexual experiences in the world! But if I promised that, I would be misleading you.[1]

Many well-meaning authors and pastors have promised that very thing, resulting in deep disappointment. What they miss is the reality of the consequences of sin. Sadly, one's past always comes into play when a couple gets married. Consider a newly married couple. Perhaps one of them has had five sexual partners and the other one had none, or perhaps both have had a high number of sexual partners. Or what if they always heard that sex is bad, dirty, and wrong until marriage? Their whole lives they heard this message, and then on their wedding day, are they supposed to instantaneously embrace the positive message of sex? And then there are those who have been violated, emotionally, physically, and spiritually. All of these scenarios have unique implications for their sex life. The message of sexual faithfulness does not magically make all these implications go away.

There are many factors that play into a couple's intimate life. So to make the blanket statement, "If you wait until marriage or if you recommit to sexual faithfulness, you will have the best sex ever," can be harmful. The reality is that no one knows how one's past will play out in their marriage. That is why God has gifted counselors to help couples work through relational issues. That is why God has given us the community

> **Share This**
>
> There are many factors that play into a couple's intimate life. So to make the blanket statement, "If you wait until marriage or if you recommit to sexual faithfulness, you will have the best sex ever," can be harmful.
>
> #everyonelovessex

of faith to come alongside us and encourage us. Regardless of the situation we find ourselves in, our responsibility is to be faithful. We are to trust God; trust that he is good. And trust that no matter what happens here, we have the promise and the hope of a better future.

Please do not misunderstand me. I am not suggesting that God cannot bring miraculous healing—because he can! However, more often than not, what I have seen in relationships is God showing up and helping a couple *through* their struggle—not magically erasing it altogether. Some of my most rewarding moments are to see couples with severe issues trust God in the midst of their struggles and see God powerfully at work. The result is that they are much stronger because they allowed God to work *in* and *through* the process.

The Test-Drive

One of the main rebuttals to being sexually faithful is that many believe you have to be "sexually compatible" in order to have a thriving relationship. Therefore, if that is the case, it follows that having multiple sex partners (whether in a committed relationship or not) is beneficial to finding one's future spouse. It is the idea that we would not buy a car without first test-driving it, so why would we marry someone without first being sexually intimate to see if we are compatible? After all, a relationship is much more valuable than a car—isn't it?

The real motive behind the statement "You have to test-drive it before you buy it" is the assumption that sex is the ultimate part of a relationship. That is, without sex you cannot have a good relationship. Sex is extremely important in a relationship. It brings couples closer together and allows couples to express their love and commitment to each other. However, there are a number of couples who cannot have sex for whatever reason—should they stop being in a relationship? Of course not. But why? Because sex is not the be-all and end-all of all things. It is important, but what is *even more important* is the relationship between the couple.

Let's put another twist on this age-old thought. Imagine you and your spouse-to-be at the altar have never had sex with anyone. The two of you can explore this great gift together. On the other hand, imagine if you followed the "test-drive before you buy" philosophy and you have had a lot of sexual partners. The more sexual partners, the more chance for issues and problems in the future. Let's consider that scenario.

If you have had multiple partners, be prepared to have that awkward conversation with your future spouse-to-be. You will have to answer questions like these: "How many people have you slept with?" "What are you ashamed of?" Imagine right now that you had to answer those questions. What would you say? On the other hand, imagine your partner had an even more elaborate list to share; how would that make you feel? (And we have not even addressed the sexual "comparison" game played in the mind.) My point is that we should treat others—in every way, including sexually—as we would like to be treated.

Imagine you had a daughter. How far would you want someone to go with her sexually? What about your sister; how far would you want someone to go with your sister sexually? Most everyone would answer those questions by saying, "I would never want anyone violating my daughter or sister sexually." But there is a disconnect here; we will go as far as possible sexually and not think twice. Perhaps we need to change our perspective.

Your future spouse is out there somewhere. Imagine your future spouse going for the proverbial "test-drive." Does that bother you? Would that frustrate you? Why? It would frustrate all of us, because we would not want anyone taking our spouse for a "test-drive." If you don't want someone else doing it with the person you want to marry, then the logical step is to live by the same standard.

The test-drive metaphor does not follow logically if we want to be in a committed, monogamous relationship. We give ourselves the best possibility of longevity when we are committed to each other—not sleeping around. To close the loop on this metaphor, let's think about the fact that the test-drive does not reveal everything there is about the car. After all, a test-drive only lasts as long as a drive around the block. How can anyone know if the car has internal issues, a head gasket leak, driveshaft problems, or frame damage? There is no way to know. But when you do buy the car—and realize that the car does not perform perfectly—you will make whatever adjustments are necessary to keep the car in tip-top shape.

> **—Share This—**
> The test-drive metaphor does not follow logically if we want to be in a committed, monogamous relationship.
> #everyonelovessex

Sex before marriage is not a necessity for a good marriage—in fact, it often leads to future issues. When two people marry, they have the privilege of learning how to be intimate with each other. Sex is something that has to be learned—and couples committed to each other have a more satisfying relationship. Sex is always the best when couples are close relationally. In other words, healthy relationships equal good sex. However, this is not always the case. In some cases, couples will have to go to specialized therapy in order to work through past issues.

Fourteen years before I married Caz, I made a decision to wait until I was married to have sex. On our wedding day, Caz and I made a commitment to each other to remain sexually faithful. While standing at the altar, I gave Caz a bracelet that I had been wearing as a reminder of my commitment fourteen years earlier (you can see the video by clicking on the "video" tab of my blog). There was no need for the "test-drive." We will figure it all out as we share the rest of our lives together.

Where Do We Go from Here?

Throughout these pages, we have seen that God's design is displayed throughout the sciences. Since God is the Creator of the universe, this only makes sense. And when we see his design in creation, it brings hope. It brings hope because we are never left to our own devices—to figure out sexuality on our own. He has given us all that we need.

Sexual faithfulness does not mean you have to have lived a perfect life. Sexual faithfulness means that at this moment— right here, right now—you can say to God, "I want to honor you with my sexuality!" When that happens, God begins to work in and through you. You may have to start seeing a professional Christian counselor, or you may have to ask forgiveness from those you have hurt. It also means that it is imperative for you to surround yourself with like-minded friends. Friends who will encourage you, build you up, and hold you accountable.

It is true that sex is appealing—that's stating the obvious. But have you ever asked why? Like everything else, it goes back to creation. God gave us the gift of sex. But for far too many people, that gift has become anything but good. It is the story of our broken world. The hurt, pain, or suffering is not what God intended. The rape, abuse, or neglect is not what God intended. In our hurt, God is there with us. In our loneliness, God is with us. In our mental illness, God is with us. In our violation, God is with us. In everything, God is with us; we just have to look up.

God wants us to thrive! God gives life—the adversary takes it away. God gives hope and redemption—the adversary brings despair and brokenness. It's time to turn to the healing and redemptive power of God. He loves you. He hurts when you hurt—and his arms are always open for you to return to him. You are never too far gone.

When God begins the restoration process, we live as we are designed to live. We begin to have fulfilling sex lives because that is what restoration does—and that is how we were originally designed.

Loving sex more than ever is receiving the redemptive power of Jesus—and embracing it. If you are married, find healing and always honor one another by honoring your sacred marriage vows. If you are single, know that you have one of the greatest gifts awaiting you—and no matter what your future partner's past or your past, God can bring redemption.

Find redemption—find your original design—and you will be able to love sex more than ever!

> **Share This**
> Find redemption–find your original design–and you will be able to love sex more than ever!
> #everyonelovessex

CONTINUING THE DISCUSSION

1. Do you think God is bigger than your past?

2. Are you able to receive God's grace and walk in his redemption?

3. Explain what the "test drive" method is and why it can be harmful.

4. Do you want to commit to sexual faithfulness now? What can your chosen community do to hold you accountable?

Have you shared your thoughts online yet?
#EveryoneLovesSex

Note

[1] I am thankful to xxxchurch.com founder Craig Gross for his insight about this book early on. One of the comments he emphasized was to not overpromise.

Index

"Sex is powerful! You don't need a book to tell you this. All you need is puberty. However, after reading Bryan Sands's well-researched and engaging book, I now understand *why* sex is so powerful as Bryan skillfully unpacks the emotional, physiological, spiritual, and social effects of sex upon each one of us. For millennial young adults making life-defining decisions in their teens and twenties, you need to read this powerful book."

—**Paul Angone,** author of *101 Secrets For Your Twenties* and *All Groan Up: Searching for Self, Faith, and a Freaking Job!*

"As a woman, and a married woman, I'm blown away at how much Bryan is able to communicate to my heart and mind on my thoughts, actions, and behaviors, and where it all stems from. WOW! This book is powerful and *very* much needed in *all* generations. It transcends time and is a light in a dark place that has been hidden far too long."

—**Joanna Beasley,** American Idol semifinalist and Christian recording artist

"How can something so awesome produce so much pain and confusion? Bryan Sands skillfully tackles this strange tension through personal stories, humor, and a study through the biblical example. Just like fire, sex is great when practiced within the boundaries of its design. But if you've only known the pain of getting burned by sex, it's time to read this book and find out what you've been missing!"

—**Jeremy Jernigan,** author of *Redeeming Pleasure*

"In *Everyone Loves Sex,* Bryan Sands dives deep into a profound exploration of sex and its potential for God-honoring connectedness through faithfulness or isolating, relational dysfunction. Through personal stories and copious research, this book takes a raw look at an essential topic for today."

—**Megan Fate Marshman,** Director of Women's Ministries at Hume Lake Christian Camps, Associate Dean of YouthMinAcademy.com, coauthor of *7 Family Ministry Essentials*

"Incredible insight! As a marriage and family therapist, I am thrilled to have a new tool to share with those we work with that helps them understand the 'why' behind the 'what' of sexual faithfulness. As a parent of four, I am beyond excited to share this with all of our young-adult children! I believe twenty years from now, the truth of this message will be noted as a true 'game-changer' for the next generation!"

—**Tammy G. Daughtry**, MMFT Founder, Co-parenting International and The Center for Modern Family Dynamics, author of *Co-Parenting Works!: Helping Your Children Thrive After Divorce*

"Out of his passion to see young people thrive, Bryan has written a wonderfully insightful, eye-opening, engaging, and challenging book which encourages the reader to think differently—and then think again—about our current sexual cultural ethic they're growing up with. Rooted in research, biblical engagement, powerful story telling, and Bryan's unique style of writing, I recommend *Everyone Loves Sex* to anyone who wants to discover God's life-giving vision for relationships and sex. Why settle for less?"

—**Matt Summerfield,** CEO Urban Saints United Kingdom, author of *Don't Make History Change the Future*

"Bryan Sands has written a much needed book that boldly and bravely addresses a topic on most people's minds—sex. This is a must read book for those who desire God's blessings and fulfillment in every area of their lives."

—**Tim Storey,** pastor, celebrity life coach, author of *Comeback & Beyond*

"Bryan Sands is a man of integrity. He lives what he speaks and writes. You will be challenged and blessed by what he shares."

—**Joe Grana,** Dean at Hope International University, author of *What God Thinks of Kids*

"Bryan Sands gets it! We need a new framework for discussing sex and the integrity of relationships, which are on the line more than ever. Bryan is asking us to enter into an honest conversation about sex and topics that have long been considered taboo in the Christian community. But we need to talk about them because youth and children are discussing them at such a young age with very little guidelines on what to do. Let's talk and drive the conversation so that we can impact the next generation to live with what Bryan calls, 'sexual faithfulness.'"

—**Gayla Cooper Congdon,** Founder of Amor Ministries, author of *Disrupted: Cultivating A Mission-Focused Life*

"Bryan is walking energy. His contagious enthusiasm for life, his family, and his faith are reflected in the pages of his new book. Faithfulness pays off in every area of life, but perhaps no more so than in the most intimate of relationships. Get ready to be encouraged and freed up by Bryan's fresh look at sex."

—**Bob Reeve**, Lead Pastor, The Cause Church, Brea, California

"This project will help all young people see the importance and benefits of sexual faithfulness. Exploring current proven studies will challenge any young person in the area of sexual activity before marriage. This much needed and valuable life resource will help countless lives. Discussion around this topic is much needed and I believe God-timed and -ordained."

—**Darren McMahon,** Director/Presenter of Your Dream School
Chaplaincy & Seminar Programs, Australia

"Bryan Sands is a great communicator with some excellent insights on personal relationships and human sexuality. His scholarly assessment of 'sexual faithfulness' brings fresh insight on a topic that affects pretty much everyone. Both the religious and nonreligious will find Bryan's research and conclusions interesting, helpful, and highly encouraging."

—**Dan Brooks,** Commander, West Covina Police Dept. (ret.)

"Bryan Sands stirs up all kinds of thoughts, emotions, conversations, and experiences with *Everyone Loves Sex,* and makes you want to be a part of the conversation. Bryan's research, insight, and candidness, makes this conversation easy to have, but also poignant and meaningful."

—**Peace Amadi,** psychology professor, Nonprofit Director of the Ruby Project, TedTalk speaker